W9-AXD-909

"LOVE ALWAYS WINS . . .

Sometimes it just takes a little longer. You can learn to perfect love in this life, or the next one, or maybe the one after that. What are a few more lifetimes more or less?"

—DICK SUTPHEN

Psychic researcher, skilled hypnotist, and lecturer, Dick Sutphen has appeared on many major television shows, and performed the first nationally broadcast past-life regression on Tom Snyder's NBC *Tomorrow Show*. With his wife, Trenna, he conducts past life regression seminars each year throughout the United States.

Books by Dick Sutphen

You Were Born Again to Be Together
Past Lives, Future Loves

Published by POCKET BOOKS

Dick Sutphen

Past Lives, Future Loves

PUBLISHED BY POCKET BOOKS NEW YORK

Another *Original* publication of POCKET BOOKS

POCKET BOOKS, a Simon & Schuster division of
GULF & WESTERN CORPORATION
1230 Avenue of the Americas, New York, N.Y. 10020

ISBN: 0-671-83485-1

First Pocket Books printing August, 1978

10 9 8 7 6 5 4

POCKET and colophon are trademarks of Simon & Schuster.

Printed in the U.S.A.

A few of the names in this book have been changed in cases where the subjects would prefer to remain anonymous.

Special thanks to Joanne Ordean, Richard Bach, Kingdon Brown, Chethlahe and Kandy, and especially to my editor, Pat Golbitz, who keeps me on the right track.

To
Neeta and the Tribe

the
drumbeats
continue
to
echo

CONTENTS

A Note from the Author 13
1. The Atlantis Regression 17
2. The Paranormal Dream 30
3. The Higher-Self Session and the Technique
   Dream 37
4. The Identity Transference 41
5. Individual Parallel Sessions 51
6. Parallel Seminar Sessions and Additional
   Input 56
7. Case History: A *Meta*physical Examination 67
8. Other Concepts of Reincarnation 90
9. Karma Without the "Hocus Pocus" 104
10. The Kingdon Brown Session 111
11. Psychic Abilities and Guidance 119
12. Case History: Bob and Mary—Past Life
    Regression and Physical Healing 130
13. Case History: Charlotte—Seminar
    Regression 142
14. Case History: Carl and Bettye—Chakra
    Link 152
15. Love, Peace and Problems 162
16. Case History: Ben and Christina 167

17. My Own Case History: The Ed Morrell
    Story   176
18. Eileen and Pat and the "Light People"   190
19. The Frequency Switch—Another Concept
    beyond Reincarnation   204
20. Supportive Material from the Doctors   213
21. Who Needs Awareness?   219
22. Future Freedom—Creating Your Own
    Reality   222
23. Shielding and Protection Techniques   241
24. A Love Story   249

A NOTE FROM THE AUTHOR

In my last book, *You Were Born Again to Be Together* (Pocket Books, 1976), I recorded the results of many years of research into the past lives of mates and lovers. It is my sincere belief that everything in that volume is reality.

- The metaphysical belief in reincarnation and karma is basic to the nature of reality. Reincarnation is the cycle of rebirth on the earth plane, and we will continue to be born over and over again until we evolve beyond the need of earthly experiences. Karma (cause and effect) is a belief system of total justice. It states that we and we alone are responsible for everything that happens to us. We created our present circumstances by what we did in the past and how we live our present life will dictate our future.
- Men and women who share, or have shared, an important relationship in this life have been together in previous lifetimes. These past ties usually explain their present circumstances.
- Love does not die—it cannot die, for it is not limited to the physical boundaries of time and space.
- Incompatibility, fighting and divorce are only temporary setbacks. They are learning experiences necessary

13

to achieve harmony and to overcome fear, which is the opposite of love. The bond between a man and a woman will continue as an exploration of their combined potential throughout their spiritual evolution.

You Were Born Again to Be Together provided numerous documented case histories showing that love is immortal. Metaphysical ideas were woven throughout the pages, making the philosophy easy to understand. Once it was mailed off to the publisher, I started to work on some entirely new psychic research projects. Yet, all paths seemed to keep circling back to the man/woman bond. Before *You Were Born Again to Be Together* was even released to the bookstores, it was evident to my wife Trenna and me that we were being directed into further exploration of the same subject. New doors were opening that expanded our existing knowledge, and although we didn't always understand the true meaning of what we were receiving and experiencing, we continued to explore. Sometimes there were months between receiving and our understanding the importance of the communications and regressions.

When it is time for new awareness to be released from the nonphysical to the physical realms, I believe that it is channeled through many people at the same time. I don't know why Trenna and I, and those associated with us, have been chosen as one of these channels, but we certainly welcome the opportunity to communicate to others concepts which have become part of our own beliefs.

We are dedicated to objectivity in our research, yet we will not refrain from releasing an idea because we cannot prove it to be fact. I feel that reincarnation has been scientifically proven through research by men such as Dr. Ian Stevenson,* and through regressive hypnosis case histories which have checked out in every minute detail. But many scientists do not accept such evidence. They call it coincidence.

----

* Author of *Twenty Cases Suggestive of Reincarnation*, American Society for Psychical Research.

I was recently on a television show with Hugh Lynn Cayce, Ruth Montgomery and Gina Cerminera. As Hugh Lynn pointed out, "After coincidence and coincidence and coincidence and coincidence, when do you stop calling it coincidence?"

Trenna and I hope to take the "weird" connotations out of paranormal occurrences and psychic abilities. Everyone has a natural psychic potential. The words *esoteric, occult,* and *supernatural* have been synonymous with reincarnation, karma and psychic investigation long enough. It is time to lift the mysterious veil and bring these subjects into the sunlight. There is no such thing as "supernatural"—all is natural; there are simply some things most people do not understand. . . . and it is now time to understand. In exploring these concepts we are not delving into the occult, we are simply seeking to expand our awareness of the true nature of reality.

If past lives, parallel-lives and a sixth (psychic) sense are in fact reality, then there is a reason for these realities. There is universal law and it is certainly time to understand it, for we are here on earth living our lives for a *purpose*. Until we can comprehend that purpose and the full extent of our powers and abilities, we make our lives more difficult than they need to be.

If you believe in reincarnation, you should be ready to expand your thinking to include the concepts of the "lack of time" and "parallel-lives." I will explain these very simply. The first section of this book shows step by step, through our own experiences, how we came to accept and comprehend this aspect of what we've come to believe is reality.

If you are one of the few, but ever growing numbers, who accepts metaphysics as a philosophy of life, of love and freedom, then it is time to use wisdom to erase your negative karma and create your own reality. That is the main goal of this book; to show you through case histories, examples, analogies and interviews, how your past and parallel-lives are affecting your present life, and to show you that you have the ability to take control of your destiny, to let go of the past, and create a future of freedom and self-bestowed success and happiness.

Walk in harmony,

Scottsdale, Arizona
August, 1978

CHAPTER 1

THE ATLANTIS
REGRESSION

In August of 1975, Trenna and I were at the Arizona State University Library in Phoenix. We were researching historic background to verify information received in the hypnotic regressions I was compiling for *You Were Born Again to Be Together*. After a long day reviewing volumes of facts, we didn't feel like driving the one hundred and twenty miles back to our home in the Bradshaw Mountains, so we decided to get a motel for the night.

After an hour of swimming and relaxing around the pool, and a leisurely dinner, we were charged with energy again. As a continuation of our research, I regressed Trenna.

"We already know three past lives we've shared. I'd like to know if there are more. Maybe we could go back to the first lifetime we were together on the earth and move forward." Trenna agreed.

The following regression session was originally included in the final manuscript of *You Were Born Again to Be Together,* but my editor felt it was best to leave it out. The book was getting too long, and the lifetime took place on the lost continent of Atlantis, so there was no way of verifying the information. I feel now that she was guided to leave it out of that book because it would prove to be of much more value in this one to help illustrate some entirely new concepts about reincarnation.

TRENNA
Regression Session
August, 1975

Hypnosis induced and regression preparation completed. The following instructions were then given: "We know of three past lifetimes in which you and I have been together. I now want you to go back in time to the very first time we were together. It will be at the time of an important event early in our relationship, in our very first earth incarnation together." Instructions completed.

Q. What do you see and what are you doing at this time?
A. (Subject is laughing, a shy little giggly laugh.)
Q. I want you to speak up and tell me what is happening.
A. We're sitting in graduation.
Q. Can you describe the graduation to me?
A. It's in a giant forum; the sun is going down . . . It's outside but there is a huge dome that is suspended overhead. (Laughing.) I'm trying to be very prim. It's a very serious lecture we're receiving, but he is sending me the funniest advances I've ever heard. (Snicker.)
Q. What is he saying to you?
A. We're supposed to be controlling our telepathic thoughts, but he's evading that. I'm trying not to acknowledge him.
Q. What are these thoughts amounting to? What is he sending?
A. He's telling me . . . (laughing) that my gown isn't doing a thing for my body.
Q. How old are you at this time?
A. Eighteen.

Q. How old is he?

A. I think he's twenty.

Q. Are you attracted to him?

A. Yes, but I don't want him to know it.

Q. What are you graduating from?

A. The School of Philosophy.

Q. What will you do now that you've graduated?

A. I want to go out and work with people. I will try to attract more people to our temple.

Q. What philosophy will you be teaching?

A. The basic truths . . . that we are all one . . . He's making it very difficult.

Q. Why?

A. Because of his remarks.

Q. What are some of his other remarks?

A. He's telling me to smile if I'll agree to meet him someplace . . . and I'm trying very hard not to smile.

Q. But do you smile?

A. Yes . . . I'm going to have to go, I guess . . . I've committed myself.

Q. All right, let's move forward to the time you actually meet him. (Instructions given.)

A. He's standing on the beach . . . and I'm telling him that I got some strange looks from the teachers for my unexcusable conduct . . . and he's laughing.

Q. What else is he saying to you?

A. He's trying to tell me how nice the water is for swimming . . . and I'm teasing him . . . asking him what I'm supposed to think of my fellow philosopher.

Q. What is happening now?

A. We're swimming.

Q. Are you enjoying yourself?

A. Yes. (Laugh.)

Q. Is there anyone else there with the two of you.

A. No . . . I don't think they'd believe us.

Q. Why?

A. I don't think they'd believe us if they saw it anyway.

Q. Why?

A. We're supposed to be prim and proper, you might say.

Q. How are you being improper?

A. We are supposed to be dedicated to spiritual pursuits opposed to the body.

Q. You are required to avoid physical contact?

A. We are to devote five years dedicated to spiritual areas because we have just graduated from the school . . . to rise above our own self-interest.

Q. Why is just going swimming together wrong?

A. Because we're both interested in other ways.

Q. Are either of you wearing any clothes at this time?

A. No.

Q. Tell me what else is happening.

A. I have . . . it's getting dark now, we should return to our quarters . . . we're just walking along the beach talking . . . and making fun of our professors. We have not really been permitted to communicate telepathically through our learning processes . . . we've been playing on each other's minds.

Q. You've been playing games with each other's minds?

A. We've been sending thoughts back and forth . . . I guess you might say challenges.

Q. What kind of challenges?

A. Who can hold out five years.

Q. You mean sexually?

A. Uh huh.

Q. What else is happening?

A. He's saying good night to me at the quarters . . . We decided we'd like to try some spiritual work together first. We are going to meet out on the astral planes and work together there first.

Q. All right, let's let go of this and move forward in time to an event of importance that transpires between the two of you. (Instructions given.)

A. We're in this . . . ah . . . it's a huge building divided into many facets. . . . The professor has been probing our minds. . . . He's sorting out the people . . . the people who will carry out the different types of spiritual work.

20

Q. What are his decisions regarding you and your friend?

A. Well, he knows about us . . . nothing can be secretive here. He's telling us we must decide whether we will do our work together or separately. He's reminding us that we will be dividing our strength, our potency, by being together. We're trying to tell him that through the two of us, that we will be able to influence more people because of our love. Because of seeing us together and not as a single person.

Q. Is this sort of thing allowed?

A. Yes . . . we have this freedom.

Q. What else is happening?

A. We have decided to go together. The professor has seen the beauty in it, and he sees that we are very sincere in our beliefs.

Q. Will you be married?

A. Yes. I don't know how to describe it. It is a union on the spiritual plane.

Q. Is there a physical ceremony?

A. Not in the sense that . . . only the two of us will meet. There is a room, and we will mentally . . . I've seen them . . . they are huge round pieces of thin silver metal. They are perfectly balanced. With our minds, we will cause the pitches . . . cause the discs to vibrate. . . . As they vibrate, the two sounds will create a harmony that will be our own. That will be our union.

Q. So this is the actual physical ceremony?

A. Yes, it is the meeting of our spirits, opposed to the physical.

Q. When will this take place?

A. When we are ready. It is up to us to go to the chamber when we are ready.

Q. Is there anyone else present during this?

A. No. This is the total vibrations of two beings. Anyone else would vibrationally interfere.

Q. When this is completed, you will be married in the eyes of society?

A. We are not concerned with the eyes of society. Our spirits will be in union in the eyes of God.

Q. What country are you living in at this time?

A. Atlantis.

Q. All right, let's move forward in time once more to an event of importance that takes place in the future. (Instructions given.)

A. Such a beautiful experience. . . . We're standing across from each other. . . . The room is like a solid mirror . . . the lights . . . the lights are prisms . . . the whole room is reflecting . . . we can see a thousand faces of each other . . . a thousand faces . . . they're all spinning around . . . slowly . . . slowly bringing up the vibrations . . .

Q. Are you causing them to move with your minds?

A. Yes . . . they're vibrating . . . it's a tonal vibration . . . it's tingling . . . tingling through me . . . the whole room is just vibrating . . . (Subject's voice is faint, far away and calm.)

Q. Is there anything more about this experience you can verbally communicate to me?

A. The lights are flashing on and off . . . it's a total essence of the senses . . . the lights, colors, sound, vibrations . . . every sense is being carried to its optimum.

Q. Now this is the ceremony that joins your spirits, is that correct?

A. Yes.

Q. Are there any more details you can communicate to me about the ceremony and the difference the two of you feel now?

A. We just feel completely in tune. . . . It's like all our senses have been brought together. . . . We each have our own tonal vibration, but we have one now.

Q. How will this joint vibration be used?

A. By bringing our minds into the vibration that is part of each of us, we will be able to contact one another over great distances, we can use it for healing, by combining our powers they will become much more effective. We will be able to create a

22

healing color, and when properly directed we can use it in our spiritual work.

Q. Now you have merged spiritually upon this plane, will this also have an effect on your physical involvement?

A. Yes.

Q. Have you made love to each other before this time?

A. Yes . . . but it will not be the same after this, it will be different now . . . an experience that could only be shared between two people who have been joined as we have.

(At this point in the session I decided to try another experiment, only this time with myself. Unknown to Trenna, who was lying beside me in a deep trance, I lay down beside her and put myself into a very light trance. Light enough to continue questioning her, but under to the degree I could attempt to pick up the visual impressions of what she was receiving. This is something she often does while I'm regressing someone else and the results are usually quite impressive. When compared with the subject's visual impressions after the session, we have often found them to be identical.)

Q. All right, we are going to let go of this now, and if you do go out into the world teaching, I want you to move to the time you find yourself in this position. (Instructions given.)

A. (Trenna seems very unwilling to leave the situation she is presently reexperiencing, but when the instructions are repeated she complies.) We are talking to a group of people . . . they are asking us many questions . . . we're down in the lower parts of the city . . . the people are very poor . . . uneducated . . . the higher classes do not permit them any education . . . they think of them as worker bees to a hive . . . I believe that is a good analogy. They see them as a necessary facet of society, but not really human. We are working to convince them to rise above this by fighting for their rights to educate their children. They just . . . generation after generation . . . they can't rise above the old way of thinking.

Q. How are you dressed at this time?

A. That's what I was confused about before . . . fascinated . . . uh . . . I'm wearing a white type of helmet on my head. It comes down to a point over my nose . . . and wearing long white robes, tied above the waist with a gold tie.

Q. How is your husband dressed?

A. Very similar . . . We both carry the mark of the school, upon gold bands on our arms.

Q. What is the mark? Can you describe it?

A. It's a mark of eternity . . . I don't know how to describe it. . . . It is a line that circles back into itself . . . a symbol of rebirth . . . coming back many times . . . it now symbolizes servitude to the people.

Q. All right, I want you to remember this symbol. You will remember it even after you are awakened, and at that time you will be able to draw it for me. Will you do this?

A. Yes.

Q. I now want you to move forward in time once again to an important event in your lives, to something that takes place in the future.

A. I'm receiving two pictures again . . . we still come back to the school because our professor is held responsible for us . . . for our teachings. He must answer to the council if we create anything upsetting to the community . . . and . . . he's telling us that we are not supposed to encourage the masses . . . the lower masses . . . to revolt. That we should simply be telling our story. We are trying to explain to him . . . what good is it to tell the story if the people remain in their present positions and do not use the knowledge we are giving them?

Q. Are you in trouble at this time?

A. We will be if we continue to do so. There have

been a couple of outbreaks and they know we
have encouraged this.

Q. So what will you do now?

A. We've been thinking about. . . . We have a craft
that can transport us. . . . Then we can come back
. . . We want to continue our studies.

Q. Transport you to where?

A. The other side of the great mountains . . . there
are primitive people that we believe we can help.

Q. Are you deciding what you will do?

A. Yes, we're very torn . . . it seems so ridiculous that
our society, which is so advanced in some ways, is
so primitive in others.

Q. Let's move forward to the time you make a decision.
(Instructions given.)

A. We have to stay in the city . . . there is a . . . I
don't know . . . I can't pronounce her name . . .
Why can't I? . . . There is a seer . . . she has been
telling us that something is going to happen to the
city and we have to stay.

Q. She has been telling this to you and your husband?

A. No, she has been telling it to the council. They have
informed the professor and he has related it to us.
She is a most respected seer. I don't know if ah . . .
oh . . . I can see them . . . hordes of people . . .
they're running . . . oh they're running inland . . .
Their faces are just distorted, panicked . . . their
faces are so distorted . . . the vibrations actually
come through the skin . . . we can pick them up . . .
what they are feeling comes through and we can
see it stronger than others . . . that's why they
look so distorted.

Q. Why are they so afraid?

A. A tidal wave . . . we're above it . . . the temple
sits on top of a hill . . . and we're watching the
people running . . . we are not afraid . . . it is
destined . . . it is time for new beginnings.

Q. Has the tidal wave hit yet?

A. It has destroyed most of the city . . . the people
are clawing up the mountain side . . . the water

is coming up . . . we've decided to leave our bodies.

Q. Why?

A. We know that everyone will soon perish . . . we're leaving.

Q. Why will your bodies perish, are you not safe up on the hill?

A. The water will soon reach the hill . . . it's only a matter of time, the earth is sinking and the water is coming.

Q. So you're leaving and you know you will not return to your physical bodies?

A. No, we will meet on the spiritual plane.

Q. All right, you are now watching this from the spiritual plane and I want you to tell me what is happening.

A. The people are all drowning . . . we feel detached from what is happening . . . there was so much corruption going on in every level of society . . . corruption within the high political structure . . . turmoil between the workers and ah . . . it is simply time for new beginnings.

(End of hour and forty-five-minute session.)

When Trenna awoke, she proceeded to illustrate and explain what she had seen while in the trance. She said she had picked up much more knowledge than had been verbally transmitted while in regression. So we mixed some tall tequila and tonics and went out by the pool to discuss the Atlantian lifetime in more detail.

"During the last half of the session I went under myself," I explained. "I received strong visual impressions of what you were telling me about."

We proceeded to compare notes and found them identical, but saw some of the situations from a different perspective.

"Tell me more about what you picked up."

"Well, to begin, I seemed to know we had gone through several lifetimes prior to being educated in the

School of Philosophy. No one was there by random choice. The knowledge of past lives was general at that time, and the proper incarnations were necessary, almost like required prerequisite courses in college. That's why an eighteen-year-old could be a respected philosopher.

"The Atlantian rulers at the time were very resentful of the school, but the school itself was such an ancient and accepted part of the society that they didn't dare act openly against it. Yet with an excuse, such as in our case of promoting education among the people, the weight of authority came down. I had the feeling that those in the ruling position felt it desirable to control only a few well educated people, while dictating to the unknowledgeable masses.

"When I mentioned going across the mountains to teach, I was receiving two pictures of transportation vehicles. The primary one was a craft . . . a disc-shaped craft. Two people could fit in it, and when they were sitting down, it would come up to their waists. I don't feel it had much power or any great speed, but it would hover and move about four feet off the ground. I believe it was capable of reversing gravity.

"Another interesting thing was the dome over the forum. There didn't seem to be any supports holding it up, yet it remained suspended above our heads. I recall looking out, seeing the ocean and feeling the sea breeze while sitting in the graduation ceremony."

"Anything else?" I asked.

"One thing really sticks in my mind. All the people running up the hill in terror. I know I was seeing more than their physical faces. I think it was a situation of being able to see an aura of fear coming through the outer skin, and the result was a hideous distortion of reality.

"I know we had the ability to leave our bodies at will—to move between the physical and spiritual planes, as was evidenced at the end by leaving before experiencing physical death.

"There is another aspect to all of this that is really interesting to me. Remember how many times I've

27

told you that I've picked up the impression of a young man with curly blond hair appearing over your face? It's happened when we've been doing 'faces' (staring at each other over a candle) and quite often when I've been watching you do a regression in dim light. I've blanked my stare, and the other face has come in. I always thought it was a young Greek, but tonight in the regression, it was you back in Atlantis."

We talked for awhile, comparing our knowledge of the lost continent received through other regressions over the years with the evening's experience. They all fit together. The vast majority of subjects I've regressed when instructed, "to return to a life on Atlantis, if indeed you experienced such an incarnation," have been able to do so. Often, although they have no conscious knowledge of the civilization, information has been provided which has correlated with known facts and helped to substantiate other case histories. I believe most of us now living in the United States are ex-Atlantians who have returned at this time because we function well in the accelerated vibrations of an advanced age.

Only a few weeks before I had regressed a friend of mine. Trenna had not been present, and I hadn't discussed it with her, yet he had experienced a death on Atlantis in very much the same way we did. When I instructed him under hypnosis to move forward in time to the last day of his life, he saw himself by the sea and explained that he had come there to die. Although a very old man in fine health, he said his work was completed and it was time to leave. He had come to the sea because he loved it and spent the day absorbing the environment. At sunset he simply left his body and moved into spirit.

In May, 1976, we were in Excelsior, Minnesota, visiting my brother Bob and his wife. We decided to do some regression work one evening, and Bob was the subject. One of the lifetimes he relived was on Atlantis and he too experienced the same situation Trenna described as the water was coming up. Although he had no knowledge of our regressive experience or the mode of dress, he described the situation and death experience almost identically.

Because of these examples of individuals on Atlantis experiencing death by leaving their bodies at will, I decided to carry all Atlantian regression subjects through death and into spirit. Nineteen seventy-six was a very active year of work, both individually and in numerous past life hypnotic regression seminars Trenna and I conducted in Scottsdale and other major cities.

I now have eighteen examples of this phenomenon. None of the subjects had any prior understanding of my reasons for having them experience this death while in regression. There were many other Atlantis regressions in which death was experienced in the normal way.

We have come to the basic conclusion that only during a period of the very highest psychic evolvement did this transpire. The Atlantis civilization lasted approximately forty thousand years. Nine thousand were probably at an advanced evolutionary level.

CHAPTER 2

THE PARANORMAL DREAM

January, 1976: The alarm clock went off at 7:30 and I managed to make my way downstairs to pour a cup of instant coffee, which I carried back to bed. While sipping my way back into reality, Trenna woke up beside me. "Oh God . . . I've been having the most realistic dream . . . Jeeze!" she muttered, still half asleep.

We often lie in bed talking for awhile before arising. I offered to share my coffee, and as she reached for the cup she jerked and fell backwards. "My back . . . my back aches like I don't believe!"

Trenna is a very healthy woman in her mid-twenties who has never experienced any form of back trouble. She explained that she could not recall anything which might have caused it. I proceeded to give her a hearty back rub and asked about the dream.

"All I can remember is that I was in a room with straw on the floor and really afraid. I was holding an unusual looking symbol that hung around my neck, and I kept repeating this sound . . . like ah, 'tee-humm, tee-humm, tee-humm' . . . almost like a mantra. That's it. But the fear was so strong."

A few minutes later we both climbed out of bed. "For heaven's sake, look at my feet!" Trenna exclaimed. "Where did that come from?"

"Looks like you've been walking through mud," I answered.

"Well, I took a bath before I went to bed last night and they sure weren't in that condition when I climbed into bed," she snapped back.

"Maybe you sleepwalked," I replied, not paying much attention.

"I've never sleepwalked in my life, and if I had, where would I have walked in something like this? It's an oily black film."

My interest was now aroused. We live in the woods, and pine needles or brown mud is the only ground cover in miles. Besides, if she had gotten up during the night I'd have been aware of it . . . climbing out of our waterbed creates major waves. The substance was pitch black and resisted removal. While Trenna climbed into the bathtub, I checked the bed sheets. They were perfectly clean.

After fifteen minutes, she emerged from the bathroom. "It was worse than trying to get off paint," she said. "What do you suppose that was all about?"

"I don't know, but I'd like to find out. Maybe through hypnosis if you'd like to try."

After breakfast we went out to the hypnosis room in the building adjacent to our house. I proceeded to induce a deep hypnotic trance, then clicked on the tape recorder:

Q. In the memory banks of your subconscious mind there is a memory of everything that has ever happened to you . . . every thought, every action, every deed . . . every waking and sleeping moment of this life or any other lifetime you have ever lived. I now want you to go back in time to last night . . . to the situation which caused your feet to be covered with the black film. (Instructions given.) Speak up now and tell me what you are perceiving at this time.

A. A man . . . he's standing at the top of our temple . . . the sun is directly behind him . . . it's almost

31

illuminating his body. He's wearing a huge head-
dress . . . red and yellow feathers.

Q. What are you doing?

A. I'm standing at the bottom . . . many people around
. . . I'm holding a scroll.

Q. Tell me about the scroll.

A. It is that which our ancient ancestors passed on to
us.

Q. What is the importance of the situation in which
you now find yourself?

A. This is the day . . . I'm supposed to . . . I'm supposed to take the scroll to the top of the temple.

Q. To the man on top of the temple?

A. Yes.

Q. Tell me more of what is happening.

A. The people are all dressed in their finest ornaments.
We are in a state of reverence.

Q. Can you tell me where you are, your country, or
the name of your people?

A. Our name is a musical sound. (She hums a word
that is hard to make out on the tape.) Our ancestors came to this place from the sea . . . they
found this land . . . I am many generations from the
landing people.

Q. Tell me more of what is happening at the temple.

A. There is music . . . and the music creates a very
high tension . . . we are worshiping the coming.

Q. Tell me about the coming. Who is coming?

A. Our God . . . he's coming . . . we have been told
by the messengers that he is acknowledged . . .
the messengers of the sea.

Q. Can you describe your buildings to me, the structures?

A. Most of us live underground . . . but we have many
temples to honor our God. I must walk to the top of
our temple.

Q. Is this a ceremonial situation?

A. Yes.

Q. All right, let's move forward to the time you actually walk to the top of the temple. (Instructions
given.) Tell me what is happening.

A. There's a fire . . . I saw the smoke from the bottom, but I didn't realize . . . I . . . it is the order that I walk across these coals . . . then give the scroll to our ruler. I have to believe . . . I have to believe that I will not be harmed . . . and I will not. I know . . . I have been trained to do this . . . this is the final test . . . this will determine the good or the evil . . . I'm very scared on the inside, but I cannot show this . . . I must remain silent . . . I must believe.

Q. I want you to tell me about the experience of walking on the coals.

A. I'm standing there . . . and I must . . . I must take that step. (Long pause.) It's like I've left my body . . . I'm watching . . . my body is walking over the coals . . . and I'm watching . . . I'm almost freezing (Trenna begins to tremble.) . . . I'm above and I'm looking down. Now I'm across . . . I'm across . . . to the top of the temple . . . a space about four feet wide and about seven feet long . . . filled with hot coals . . . I walked across it and I'm not hurt . . . I'm handing the scroll to him. He's accepting it . . . very happily.

Q. What is happening now?

A. The people are cheering . . . and the music is stopped. It was almost ear-piercing music. It almost hurt. The people are cheering . . . I'm walking down the temple steps . . . I'm seeing from such a different . . . a different state than that of the others . . . because of raising myself to the ability to walk over the coals. The people are screaming but it is muffled . . . I hardly hear it . . . like it is bouncing off an invisible barrier between myself and the people.

Further questioning uncovered the following facts:

1. In the reality Trenna was experiencing she had been psychically trained for her position in that society.

2. After the experience on the temple she began to receive visions of a forthcoming tragedy. She believed that it was not their God who was coming, but a large group of men who would destroy their civilization.

3. She tried to warn the people of this and painted large red symbols of protection on the buildings. The ruler considered her a fanatic and she was sealed in a windowless room with straw on the floor.

4. In an attempt to survive she used her training to meditate in a yoga-like position. Holding the spiritual symbol of her society, she repeated the sacred words "tee-humm." After many days without food or water she experienced physical death.

5. From the nonphysical spiritual realms she was able to explain that her civilization had indeed been ravaged by an invasion and was virtually destroyed.

At this point I decided to use Higher-Self hypnosis in an attempt to further clarify the situation. This is a matter of taking a deeply hypnotized subject into the superconscious levels of his own mind. The God-self. Trenna had successfully worked in this realm on several previous occasions. The instructions were given and I began the questioning.

Q. From the level you have now attained you have the ability to answer any question I ask of you. I want to know why your back was hurting so badly this morning.

A. While incarcerated, I sat in a meditation posture . . . for so long. There was very little air. I was trying to reduce my body intake . . . so I could live longer. Hoping they would come and get me before it was too late. I hoped they would realize I spoke the truth.

Q. I want you to explain what you experienced last

night. Was this simply a dream, and if so how did you experience the physical effects?

A. This is a civilization that did exist. That does exist. I accepted the role and exchanged it in time. It could be looked back upon as history or as a creation of "now." Now is our history. A parallel reality. My conscious mind interpreted, in a distorted way, what I remembered upon waking this morning. In reality it was not a frightening experience. The pain in my back was psychosomatic and will be gone upon awakening. Millions of people have psychosomatic problems . . . psychical disorders caused only by emotional influences, which in many cases come from other lifetimes. The black film on my feet was a chemical manifestation. There was so much mental intensity in the coal walking experience that my mind produced a physical effect. The mind is all powerful and consciously limited only by the perimeters of belief.

(End of hypnosis session.)

Before awakening Trenna, I instructed her to remember every detail of what she had experienced in the trance, and gave her the posthypnotic suggestion to draw pictures of the spiritual symbol, the ruler's costume and the temple building after she awoke.

The temple seemed to be similar to structures found in ancient Mexico. Although the civilization's musical name is unfamiliar, it is a known fact that there are still numerous undiscovered ruins in that area. Many date back thousands of years, and are now completely buried. In regard to the symbol, variations of the cross have been used throughout known history, although I'd never seen a version with four prongs (or fingers of a hand) curving forward.

At the time we attempted to draw no further conclusions from this experience. Trenna's backache was completely gone after she came out of hypnosis. "It

35

seems that since I am aware of the cause, I no longer need to carry the effect," she explained.

Follow-up notes: Over the years of performing past-life hypnotic regressions, I've often found individuals reexperiencing lifetimes in an area or country similar to Atlantis and pre-Conquistador Mexico, yet the data received was pertinent to neither of these known civilizations. I have come to the conclusion that very highly developed civilizations existed in what we now call Mexico from at least 10,000 B.C. to what history records as the Mayan, Toltec and Aztec periods. Their lineage was Atlantian.

It is interesting to note that eight months after Trenna's experience, Ruth Montgomery's book *A World Before* was released. In it Ruth mentions that civilization after civilization is buried layer upon layer in Mexico. This fact is also substantiated by Mexican geologists I've talked to.

In *The World Before,* Ruth also touches upon many facts, received through Arthur Ford, Lilly and the group that helps her write her books, about Atlantis and Lemuria which I have been receiving from subjects in past life regression for years. Such cross-verification is gratifying.

CHAPTER 3

THE HIGHER-SELF SESSION AND THE TECHNIQUE DREAM

April, 1976: For about two months Trenna had been awakening in the morning with hazy memories of dreams or some form of contact through which she felt she was being taught. "It's as though I'm in an intensive learning period or going to school. I recall only scattered fragments, like a dream, but unlike a dream somehow. Even during the day, sometimes when I'm relaxing I seem to pick up flashes of what has transpired . . . or maybe something taking place right now. I don't know."

Then one afternoon in late April she asked me if I'd do a Higher-Self hypnosis session. "Take me up there, then simply let me talk. Maybe I can gain some more understanding of what is really going on."

I was busy at the time, so we decided to do the session that evening. A writer friend and his lady stopped by shortly before we started the hypnosis work. He was quite familiar with my research and had written about it for several publications, so we welcomed their witnessing this area of exploration.

Trenna relaxed in front of the fireplace on the living room floor. I induced very deep hypnosis and moved her into the Higher-Self: "You have the power and ability to move up into the highest levels of your own mind . . . the all-knowing, God level of your superconscious mind, and from this realm of expanded awareness you have the ability to look upon your life from a completely detached perspective. You have the ability to tap knowledge that is normally unattainable to your conscious mind. This is a level of total peace, total love, total freedom . . . the all-knowing psychic levels of your own mind. I am calling in your own Masters and Guides to be with you and to aid you as you move into this beautiful mental realm . . . and as you verbally communicate from your own Higher-Self. All right, you are now letting go and beginning to rise up . . . not feeling your body at all. (Instructions given.) You are now in the highest levels of your own mind and when and if it is desirable to do so, I want you to speak up and talk to me about anything you are perceiving."

(Several minutes pass.)

Trenna: There is new awareness. There is contact on a level unknown before. There is no past . . . no future . . . all is NOW. Everything is happening right now. There is no history, for history is NOW. It is only as perceived by each individual and related to his own spiritual lineage. This reality is but one of the potentials being explored in the constant "now" by my soul. Each portion of the exploration, the separate-selves experiencing parallel realities are part of the complete soul, just as the complete soul is part of the group soul known as mankind. All individual, yet all part of the whole. We are one. We are each God . . . and the combined total is God. Each cell in our physical body carries the sum total of our knowledge . . . our essence. Complete in itself, yet part of the complete body.

Look upon your lives as a multilevel chess board. Each level of the board represents a lifetime . . . a potential of exploration. You have one chess man or more on each level. This is you. Now think of each level as glass and look down upon it from above. It appears as one standard chess board. (See illustration.) You see many individual figures but they are all you . . . the kings, queens, knights, pawns . . . each is you in a different lifetime. You in many past lives, you in

38

your present life and you in future lives. Every move on any level has an effect upon the other levels—just as moving one chess man in a chess game has an effect upon the total game. This is quite easily understood as "karma," relating it to your present perception of sequential time, but this does not allow a complete understanding of the true nature of reality. For there is no time. All is transpiring now. One big chess game and every move on the varying levels of the total board is affecting the other levels of the board. The concept of karma is valid, the concept of reincarnation is valid . . . and by opening new doors of understanding you will soon begin to perceive the total picture. What seems contradictory and beyond present comprehension will soon become clear.

Athenna is a teacher. She is I and I am she. She exists on Atlantis and the learning experienced in sleep, and sometimes consciously, is preparatory for forthcoming awareness.

(End of Higher-Self session.)

In listening to the tape recording of the session both Trenna and I immediately discerned the change in her voice. It was unlike the voice pattern we normally associate with her hypnotic trances. At the time we dismissed it as the result of having reached a higher mental level than that which we normally work within.

May, 1976: I awakened twice during the night, each time fully aware of a hypnotic technique that was filling my mind. A technique I was totally unfamiliar with and one which would direct a hypnotized subject to transcend levels of consciousness and step outside of themselves . . . allowing one of their separate-selves to verbally channel through their vocal cords. This would result in a direct communication from a parallel reality. Intensified spiritual protection was required. The technique continued to flow through my mind . . . over and over, until shortly before dawn I recall myself awakening and almost yelling, "I have it, I have it, please let me get some rest!"

The next morning was Sunday and I explained to Trenna what I'd experienced during the night. She immediately volunteered as the subject to try out the technique.

"I think it's meant for us . . . at least for right now," I said. "I have a feeling if it works, it may pull a lot of loose ends together."

That afternoon Trenna relaxed in the recliner in the hypnosis room. I induced a deep trance and intensified the spiritual protection.

The soul (Oversoul: the essence of you and all of your parallel-selves in the past, present and future) decides to explore potentials on the earth plane of existence. This amounts to several lifetimes at one time. Think of the earth as a multilevel chess board.

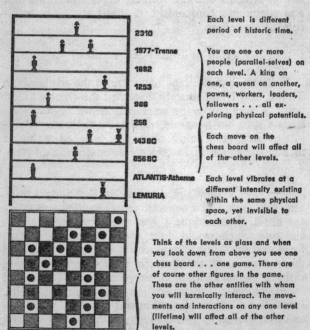

2310 — Each level is different period of historic time.

1977-Trenna
1892
1253 — You are one or more people (parallel-selves) on each level. A king on one, a queen on another, pawns, workers, leaders, followers . . . all exploring physical potentials.
986
258

143BC — Each move on the chess board will affect all of the other levels.
856BC

ATLANTIS-Athenna — Each level vibrates at a different intensity existing within the same physical space, yet invisible to each other.
LEMURIA

Think of the levels as glass and when you look down from above you see one chess board . . . one game. There are of course other figures in the game. These are the other entities with whom you will karmically interact. The movements and interactions on any one level (lifetime) will affect all of the other levels.

40

CHAPTER 4

THE IDENTITY
TRANSFERENCE

Dick: All right, you have the power and ability to allow a unique transference to take place. Our research work and the Higher-Self contact of a few nights ago points to the fact that you are in contact with another identity, residing in a parallel reality. I now want to contact this separate-self. I want you to let go and allow Athenna to come through you, to speak through you. I want you to transcend levels of consciousness and allow this to happen. (Instructions given.)

Q. I want you to speak up now and tell me your name.
A. (Long hesitation.) Athenna.
Q. Athenna, I have no knowledge of your understanding of the situation you now find yourself within, or the mental levels that you have transcended to come here. Is there anything you can tell me about this?
A. . . . I am not used to verbally communicating.
Q. Is communication achieved mentally where you come from?
A. Yes.
Q. What is your connection with Trenna? Are you aware of a tie?

A. Yes, we talk often. (She seems to be getting used to using the vocal cords.)

Q. Is this because in your reality you are more aware of such things?

A. Yes, in a sense . . . she knows intuitively . . . she meets me on the beach quite often.

Q. Is this when she is asleep? Or is this just a portion of her mind that is capable of transcending time and space?

A. Mostly when she is sleeping.

Q. Then you are teaching her? Is this correct, or helping her?

A. We are helping each other.

Q. She also helps you?

A. Yes, we talk to each other, it is like two friends— no difference. We share our problems which often run parallel with each other.

Q. Problems that run parallel?

A. Yes, I exist within an environment that is much calmer than the one you exist within. I share this mental tranquility with Trenna. She shares her emotions with me . . . allowing me to touch the emotional side of myself, rather than the extremely logical side that I pursue.

Q. I would like to be able to comprehend the exact relationship that you share with each other. Are you the same soul, or the same energy force experiencing life within two different realities? Or are you simply on a compatible frequency?

A. It is so hard to verbally communicate when you are so used to placing the thought in another's mind. I am Trenna and she is I. In sequential time as perceived by you, I will reincarnate as her. But there is no time. All exists in a constant NOW. Think of our lifetimes as a book. I am living in chapter two, Trenna in chapter fourteen, but the book is already written . . . and we are the book. We are living all the chapters at once. I am also experiencing the lifetime of a man in a very primitive society . . . that is another chapter. We are many lives which make up the entire book. I experience Trenna's lifetime as the future and she experiences mine in a past sense, although they are all happening at once.

Q. They are happening at once, simply on different levels of reality, or within different time warps?

A. Yes.

Q. You and Trenna are indeed separate-selves then?

A. Yes, we are separate-selves in one sense . . . with all of our separate-selves being the totality . . . the soul. Think of me as the seed, Trenna the seedling . . . and we are growing into a beautiful flowering plant.

Q. I like your analogy. Do you have anyone else you would consider a separate-self existing in Trenna's time-frame?

A. No, but I am in contact with those she is in contact with . . . but only through her. I can observe them and their reactions through her.

Q. Is Trenna in contact with more individuals, or separate-selves other than yourself . . . others existing within different realities?

A. Yes, but she is not consciously aware of this. She is just beginning to become aware.

Q. Is this the case with everyone?

A. Intuitively, yes. We are all subconsciously in contact with our separate-selves . . . we are like a sponge. We absorb many, many contacts when we need them. As an example, when you sit down and start to paint, you tap in on many different people around you . . . . I have a very strange feeling.

Q. Can you explain this to me?

A. Trenna's structural makeup is very different than mine and I'm not used to . . . I am feeling the effects of her body and mind and the chemicals are much different . . . they are affecting me.

Q. Can you continue to speak to me, or would you prefer . . .

A. I'm all right, I can continue to communicate.

Q. Can you tell me about your reality . . . the place where you live?

A. I live in Atlantis in the city of Alturia.

Q. What do you do in Atlantis? How do you spend your time?

A. My work is largely healing . . .

Q. Trenna and I experienced a past life, when we were living on Atlantis. Was that lifetime the life you are now living, Athenna?

A. Yes, it was.

Q. Then I too have a portion of my own identity . . . a separate-self who is experiencing life on Atlantis at this time?

A. Yes, Dick, you are Mark in my reality, and we are now together, just as you and Trenna are together in your own reality. Mark works with you quite often. (She hesitates.) I am feeling such a weight, it is very hard . . .

Q. The weight will alleviate . . . on the count of three the weight will be gone. (Strong hypnotic suggestions given.)

A. I believe what I am feeling is the gravitational . . . I am not used to this much pull on my body . . . I am much lighter. My size is about the same as Trenna's, but her body feels as if it weighs three times as much as my own.

Q. Do you feel like continuing, or would you like to end this session?

A. I would like to continue.

Q. What is your age in Atlantis at this time . . . as I think of years?

A. (Hesitation.) I guess I am just trying to figure out how to best communicate with you. I have spent many lifetimes preparing for the lifetime that I am now experiencing. We are able to control what body we come back into. So in reality, I am around two hundred or so, but physically I am only twenty-six.

Q. Do you have the ability, other than through this hypnotic technique, to transfer or transcend reality at will?

A. Consciously only to a very limited degree. We all do subconsciously.

Q. You seem to recall Trenna working with you when you're out of your body or in a period of sleep.

A. Yes . . . I know when she comes, like the times she comes to the beach . . . I'll be walking on the beach and she will be there and we will talk. She will return, or I will come to her when her mind seems to drift or is idle. I am often communicating with her. When she feels she is on "automatic," it is because we have been communicating. She has informed me that it has been very calming to her mind. She sees how everything seems to flow in its natural order when she allows positive energy to work through her. This is of course part of my logical training on Atlantis, which she is learning to apply to her life here.

Q. Can I ask you about the concept of reincarnation? Are all of the past lives we recall in hypnotic regression actually parallel existences which are presently affecting us?

A. Yes . . . but affecting you just as you always thought the past lives were affecting you. You are searching for absolute answers . . . it will take time for you to comprehend that there is no such thing. There are many ways that an entity can experience physical existence or potentials that he needs to explore to complete his cycle before returning to the nonphysical realms. . . . What is that noise?

(We were working with the windows open and a very noisy motorcycle without a muffler drove by outside.)

Q. It was a motorcycle, disregard it.

A. The environment you live within . . . I don't understand. Things like that destroy your own vibrations! (Very vehement.)

Q. Is a noise like that upsetting to you?

A. Yes . . . machines on Atlantis never carry any noise

. . . they operate with heat, light, or water in some cases . . . but we never bring anything into the environment that . . . it disarranges . . . right now I am circling.

Q. You are circling. In other words the noise of the motorcycle caused an upset of your vibrations to the point of losing your equilibrium?

A. Yes . . . it does to yours too, if you only realized it!

Q. Can you tell me anything about that?

A. Well, you are not a mass, although you appear to be a mass . . . you are floating . . . you are particles floating and vibrating against each other, and every vibration around you affects you. As an example, anytime someone enters the room, it affects your mood, your whole perception . . . everything about your vibrational field changes. Therefore, it affects you emotionally. You either respond positively or negatively. Often you do not know why you are feeling the way you do.

Q. I guess Trenna and I are aware to some degree. We felt by moving into the woods in the mountains we could function much more effectively than we could living in a city.

A. I seemed to be swirling . . .

Q. Are you all right now?

A. Yes . . . I feel lighter now. I was feeling so heavy. If you are able to open yourself more, you could relate back to us. It would help you immensely in completing and accomplishing the goals that you have set out before you.

Q. How would you suggest that I might accomplish this, Athenna?

A. If you program yourself on going into hypnosis, or before going to sleep, to go back and touch upon us . . . we would be able to improve communications with you. You subconsciously know this and you are doing it whether you realize it or not . . . but the communication can be intensified and your awareness expanded.

Q. What about the other realities that we have tapped.

If you are aware of Trenna, you are probably also aware of these. The Alamos group reincarnation, the lineage from Teotihuscán.* Are these also separate realities, or parallel lives going on at this time?

A. Yes, because everything is happening now. These people are experiencing. I am not in touch with these realities for they are much closer to your vibrations than to mine.

Q. Do you know your own destiny? Trenna relived your entire life . . . or a good portion of your life, including your death in the regression.

A. Yes.

Q. What will transpire at the time you do leave your body on Atlantis for the last time?

A. I try not to think of these things for I am trying to live my potential to the best of my ability. I do realize how insignificant one lifetime really is.

Q. You spoke of reincarnation earlier . . . of many lives of preparation for the lifetime you are experiencing. Did you actually evolve by plan through a series of lifetimes to the one you are now experiencing?

A. Yes, I needed to evolve many times; and because of our knowledge, we are able to control this. I was able to learn through many lifetimes and retain the knowledge. After each lifetime I would go into the "prior life perception chamber" . . . thus assimilating all of my prior knowledge and abilities. Using this knowledge as the foundation for the new life.

Q. And you will evolve to be Trenna over many, many thousands of years?

A. She is me in her past life. I am her in my future life, but we are all existing at one time, only within different dimensions of reality. Like I said the other night through Trenna, we are a multileveled chess board and what I do, although she may be only subconsciously aware of it, affects her . . . and what

_____
* *You Were Born Again to Be Together.*

she does affects me. It is only as a grain of sand in comparison to all the other entities that we are in contact with . . . subsconsciously . . . consciously.

Q. Then it was you speaking through Trenna in the Higher-Self session the other night? That explains the unique vocal pattern?

A. Yes.

Q. Then reincarnation, as we think of it is valid? What you are saying simply expands the concept?

A. Yes, there are many words or labels that you can put on a concept and by doing that you are limiting the perspective. There are many, many answers to the questions that you ask. I'm sure there are aspects which seem contradictory, but you will soon understand.

Q. What about the dream Trenna experienced . . . the manifestation of oily black film on her feet?

A. This too was a past life, or parallel reality . . . one which she has experienced . . . is experiencing. This reality is much closer to my own and will transpire about a thousand years in my future, after the destruction of Atlantis, in the country you now know as Mexico. This would have transpired about eleven thousand years ago—in your time reference.

Q. Athenna, do you feel it is right for the concepts we are discussing to be communicated to the people existing within my reality at this time?

A. Yes, your reality is evolving towards an environment similar to that of Atlantis.

Q. How long have you been in direct or conscious contact with Trenna?

A. Only recently on the level we have been discussing. You see, as you advance your vibrational rate through expanding your awareness . . . new doors always open. Trenna has been evolving towards my vibrations . . . my frequency. It is not identical, but close enough for more conscious contact than before. She is also evolving towards the vibrations of many others. We are all atoms vibrating within a time/space. Her vibrations are now compatible

48

with mine. Thus the contact is natural. Someone else's atoms would not be so attuned.

Q. Was Trenna previously in contact with others of a lower vibration?

A. Subconsciously, but lower vibrations would not be conducive to this form of contact.

Q. Can you explain that a little more?

A. In the past Trenna and I weren't really valuable contacts to each other. Through our evolution this has changed. As an example, Trenna and I are also a primitive fisherman. I am aware of him, and I have the ability to achieve a form of conscious contact, but this would be fruitless. I would totally confuse him, and through this confusion I could harm him. He couldn't offer anything to me and I can offer very little to him.

Q. So contact would probably only take place with separate-selves within evolved societies . . . such as Atlantis, or in the future . . . hoping that my own society continues to evolve towards expanded awareness.

A. Yes, most likely . . . but not as an absolute.

Q. Let me ask you another question. Were Trenna and I destined to come together?

A. Yes, as you and Trenna are Mark and I . . . a direct lineage or extension of us, as we are of you, although I realize that is a little hard to comprehend. We have evolved many lifetimes together, but of course we are also all involved with many others in much the same way . . . in other lives, other periods of time as you think of them. I would like you to contact Mark on your own. I don't feel that through me he could be as much value to you as he could be through direct contact. His present life runs parallel to your own.

Q. Athenna, does all this fit the concepts and research which I wrote about in *You Were Born Again to Be Together*?

A. Oh yes, although you have expressed exactly what we are experiencing you didn't really realize the full implications of the concepts. You will soon

have many experiences and will make personal
contacts that will clarify what we have discussed
here today.

Q. All right, Athenna, thank you so much for working
with us. If you are willing to do it again, we will
plan on it.

A. Of course.

(End of transference session.)

Upon awakening, Trenna sat quietly in the lounge
chair for a few moments, staring at me. "That was one
of the strangest experiences I've ever had."

"What can you tell me about it?" I asked.

"Well, I felt as if I'd stepped behind myself. I was
listening to myself, but had no control over what was
coming out of my mouth. I've never experienced anything like it. I'm going to have to think about all this
for awhile."

(NOTE: It should be pointed out that there is no connection between Athenna and Athena, the Greek god-
dess, daughter of Zeus.)

CHAPTER 5

INDIVIDUAL
PARALLEL SESSIONS

THE CALINDA SESSION

September, 1976: Calinda Marshall, a thirty-three-year-old divorcee, sat deeply hypnotised in the recliner lounge. Instructions, preparation and spiritual protection were completed and the following instructions were given: "You have the power and ability to draw upon all knowledge existing in the superconscious levels of your own mind, and to allow this knowledge to flow down into the conscious mind as we work together and as I guide you to do so. If you are now also another individual existing on the earth plane, or if you have been another individual at anytime within the timeframe of your birth up until now, I want you to transfer identities with your own separate-self. If there is more than one, your mind will choose which of these simultaneous multiple incarnations you will choose to explore this afternoon. If you are experiencing only your present incarnation on the earth, you will inform me of this after the completion of the actual transfer instructions."

(Instructions given.)

Q. Can you speak up now and tell me your name?

A. Martin Frasier. (Her voice is deeper and more dominant than before.)

Q. Where do you live, Martin?

A. Los Angeles, California.

Q. What is the date today?

A. May 23, 1974. (Two-and-a-half years earlier than the current time of the transfer session.)

Q. What are you doing now, Martin?

A. I've been taking care of Sarah most of the night. Just laid down to try to get some shut-eye.

Q. Who is Sarah?

A. My wife . . . she's very sick, you know.

Q. No, I'm sorry I didn't know. What is wrong?

A. Cancer. Damn cancer!

Q. How old are you, Martin . . . how old is Sarah?

A. I'm sixty-three. Sarah is fifty-nine.

Q. What can you tell me about Sarah's condition? What are the doctors telling you?

A. I take her to the hospital for weekly treatments, but they tell me she only has a few more months.

Q. How long have you known that Sarah had cancer?

A. Let's see . . . about six months . . . yes! It's going to be so lonely without her. We've been married for forty years and four months now. We're trying to make the most of every day. It's hard . . . really hard. I want to keep her with me.

The transfer at this point seemed to begin to fade, or to lose focus in Calinda's mind. All attempts to re-establish contact proved futile in this and a later session.

This was only one of numerous explorations and test transfers we were attempting at this time and I didn't think much more about it until Calinda called me several months later.

"I had some friends in L.A. help me," she explained. "They were able to verify the death of a Sarah Frasier in September of 1974. She died of cancer in Los Angeles. They could find out nothing about her husband and he is not listed in the phone directory."

"Well, at least it is one more verification," I replied. "You know your experience has some validity. Are you sure you had no knowledge of the people or the situation before we did the transfer session?"

"Absolutely sure. I get to L.A. about once a year, but I only know a few people. There is something here that is really bothering me though, Dick. It was 1974 that my seven-year marriage to Tom really began to come apart at the seams. He claimed I was overly possessive to the point that I drove him crazy. It seemed that as he began to pull away from me, I just tried all the harder to hold him. We were divorced in November of that year. Assuming for a moment that Martin Frasier was actually my parallel-self, or one of them, could his fear of losing his wife have affected my attitudes towards Tom? You say we are probably attached to our parallel-selves on a superconscious level. What if my anxiety actually came from him, or was exaggerated by his situation . . . What does that add up to? God, not only do you have to worry about yourself, but also what some other self is doing to your head! I don't like it."

"I don't know. I certainly wish I did, because in knowing we're going to be one step closer to understanding the true nature of our individual reality. From a karmic (cause and effect) perspective it really wouldn't change any of the classic concepts. Your totality came to the earth to learn needed lessons, to explore and experience."

My answer seemed inadequate, yet it was the only one I had. It seemed to me that Trenna and I were being channeled information from the other side. Step by step, unseen higher intelligences were opening new doors to understanding, and were providing just enough substantiating data to keep us investigating. Why us? I suppose because they knew I could communicate the concepts in my writing to a segment of readers who would identify with them.

In another very complicated session involving a divorce situation, a forty-year-old male subject seemed still to be with his divorced wife, but in parallel incarnations. He saw himself and a woman he "knew" was his ex-wife living somewhere in China or east Asia. Both were in their early twenties and quite happy. The woman was living a submissive role to her husband.

"The idea that I'm still together with her is the last thing I'd like to know." He scowled at me after awakening.

"Tell me about the relationship you used to share with your wife . . . in this aspect of your reality," I asked.

"She was a dictator. I finally just had my fill and started divorce proceedings, but she fought it all the way. She'd love to have experienced this session. When I pick up the children on weekends, she is still saying that we should get back together . . . even after five years of divorce."

"If your experience in hypnosis is valid, then you decided to explore the potentials of alternate leadership roles in simultaneous marital situations," I summarized, rather unnecessarily.

Many additional individual transfer sessions followed, always using different subjects to explore the concepts. More often than not, details didn't check out, or could only be partially verified. In over two-thirds of the cases the parallel-self lived in another country. Often they had already died.

Yet there were verifications. Subjects in hypnosis accurately described other people who did exist. It doesn't prove that they are parallel-selves. I can't know for sure that the subjects didn't know about these people prior to the sessions and thus simply provided me with subconsciously retained data.

There are other possible explanations: telepathic perception could have been intensified due to the hypnotic mental state; thus they simply read the mind of someone else. As a medical fact we all have measureable brain waves. Possibly two people who share similar alpha waves, in addition to some unmeasureable frequency, could find themselves "connected" on a superconscious level. Recent laboratory tests with the brain wave synchronizer tend to support this idea.

But assuming simultaneous multiple incarnations are reality, for some of us, or all of us . '. . could you meet yourself? Of course. Fine artist and psychic channel David Paladin told me he has met one of his parallel-selves and it was a very unpleasant experience. Others have explained that the experience was fantastic, or a real bummer. There seems to have been no middle-of-the-road reactions. Not having knowingly met myself yet, I cannot speak from experience.

CHAPTER 6

PARALLEL SEMINAR SESSIONS AND ADDITIONAL INPUT

After conducting several hundred group hypnosis sessions, resulting in the past life regression of thousands of people, and completing many hundreds of tape-recorded individual regressions, it is impossible not to draw many conclusions. The first, most obvious and provable fact is that the human mind is capable of communicating historic data in vivid and accurate detail, data to which the hypnotised individual had never been consciously exposed. Second, the past lives generally relate to the person's present situation in some karmic way—there is a balance, positive or negative. Third, the important people in the present life usually can be found as other identities in one or more prior incarnations. People seem to be purposely reborn within the same time-frame and seek each other out for joint exploration or evolution.

The concept of parallel-selves or simultaneous multiple incarnations within the same historic period added a new dimension to our research work. Our first exposure to the concept came through dream/psychic/regression channels late in 1974 as we investigated the case history of Louise and Alex, which appeared in *You Were Born Again to Be Together.*

On a few occasions, I'd worked with great somnambulistic hypnosis subjects with whom several past lives have been examined in detail, and follow-up research has proven to be valid. Then the subject came up with two lifetimes transpiring in different countries within the same year. In one case, a present-day Phoenix businessman was a thirty-four-year-old farmer in Virginia in 1794, and a fifty-year-old fisherman in Italy the same year. Both men enjoyed making things with their hands—especially out of wood. These regression sessions took place several years ago; and at the time, I just threw up my hands. The subject was sure he'd tapped in on some "universal mind bank" for the accurate details he'd related, and rejected the idea that these were his past lives. Yet, today fishing is his favorite sport; he and his wife take pride in their large garden; and as a hobby, he sculpts with clay.

While directing The Hypnosis Center in Scottsdale, Arizona, we provided free open-to-the-public sessions every Wednesday night. Often "believers" brought along nonbelieving friends for the evening's activities. One of our "regulars" once talked her Mormon sister-in-law into attending on the night of a planned group past life hypnosis session. She informed me that she was there only to humor the family weirdo and had no intention of being hypnotised. I told her that was fine and we were glad to have her. Throughout my casual introduction, the woman sat and scowled at me, and continued to glare as I began the group relaxation which precludes actual hypnotic induction. No sooner had I begun the initial take down than she was out like a light—obviously a deep level subject.

This particular regression was into the lifetime just prior to the one that we're now living; and in a group situation, the subjects are asked to see the impressions as they are directed, before their own inner eyes, and to answer my questions to themselves—nonverbally. Prior to awakening, they're instructed to remember every detail of what has transpired. When the regression was completed and the group was awakened, I noticed that our disapproving guest sat almost frozen in her chair. The scowling was back but no longer directed at me. She was staring wide-eyed into space.

I began asking several in the group what they had experienced; and as usual, in turn, they related detailed stories about other times and places. Finally, my curiosity got the better of me and I directed myself to Miss Scowl: "I know you didn't plan on being regressed; but evidently you changed your mind, for as I believe you're aware—you were hypnotised. Did you receive anything that you'd be willing to share with the group?"

At this point, sister-in-law was pulling on her arm, "Come on, Diane, did you? Did you?"

The scowl deepened again as Diane responded, "Yes . . . but I don't believe a bit of it. This reincarnation stuff is absolutely ridiculous!"

"I can certainly respect your opinion, Diane," I said, "but if you did receive impressions, it might be interesting to talk about them."

"Well, the year was 1914," she began. "I was a young woman living in Chicago, Illinois; and my father delivered milk to our entire neighborhood in a horse-drawn wagon. At the age of twenty-five I married Lester Watkins, and we moved to the edge of the city . . ."

The story took her fifteen minutes to relate, and her final words were, "I died at the age of seventy-three in bed in my daughter's home. But I don't believe a bit of it."

Realizing that I had a fantastic subject, I asked her if she'd be willing to undergo a directed regression. This time I'd hypnotise only her, and from the hypnotic trance she would verbally answer me. At first she wasn't receptive to the idea; but after prodding from the group, she agreed.

Once more she quickly achieved a deep state and I began to ask her questions.

Q. What is your name?
A. Thomas Danielson. (Her voice was a thick English accent.)
Q. Where do you live, Thomas?
A. London, England.

Q. Can you tell me what year it is?
A. 1921.

That did it! I continued the extremely interesting regression; but immediately upon awakening, my subject smiled in gleeful delight, "See, I told you! How could I be two people living at the same time in two different countries. Reincarnation is a lot of nonsense."

At the time I didn't have an answer. Before leaving, she invited me to attend Sunday services at the Church of the Latter Day Saints. "I'll send you a fantastic book on Mormonism," was her parting shot. Now it was sister-in-law who was scowling.

After working with Trenna, and several others on parallel transfers, it became increasingly obvious that an "affinity-tie" usually existed between the separate-self and conscious self, whether the two existed in varying time-frames or the here and now. With Trenna it was the common interest in psychic methodologies. In another circumstance, one self was a horse race fanatic and the other raised horses. An artist friend of ours transferred to a contemporary incarnation as a dress designer in Europe. In a couple of other cases, we found diametrically opposed opposites—so opposite that it appeared purposeful and the theory here is that each could have agreed to take on opposite learning aspects. Possibly the Yin-Yang concept of duality is applicable here. Maybe those who found separate-selves with affinities would also be capable of finding opposites?

If the affinities relate and influence, how about the karmic aspects and personal behavioral patterns? If your parallel-self is having a bad day, is it affecting you? Maybe that feeling of depression that you cannot relate to a cause is coming from "another you." These are just a few of the most obvious questions and I decided to turn to my own Higher-Self for the answers. After self-inducing a deep trance and transcending levels of consciousness, Trenna directed the session and handled the tape recorder. The following is the important portion of the communication:

Each of your physical explorations influences all of your other selves, which are all co-exploring simultaneously. Physical and mental effects can be intuitively transferred from one to the other. The degree of effect would depend upon each aspect's level of awareness. One who achieves a harmonious vibrational balance is less likely to be affected than an aspect in conflict with himself. Your attunement in this area determines how any karmic situation can manifest on a physical level. Ideally, in a harmonious balance, you will learn through all of your other selves, without the necessity of negative effect. This also relates to astrological influences. You self-inflict your externally created effects and limitations by allowing your awareness to fall short of potential. Through inner harmony and environmental unity, you can transcend personal turmoil and in so doing, achieve amelioration for your totality.

Upon awakening, I was staring into Trenna's special pixie smile. "Boy that was a mouthful," she laughed. "Yeah, if I'm remembering it all, I agree! The goal does seem to be to 'get-it-together,' doesn't it?"

After considerable testing, we decided to do a group parallel-transfer session in each of our past life seminars. With over a thousand people now having experienced this experiment, we have a few more answers. Eighty to eighty-five percent of the individuals in each group received some impressions during the sessions. When I asked, "How many physical earth explorations are you now exploring or have you explored in the time-frame of your life—from birth up until now?" the highest reported number was four. Two or three was the common response. In a small percentage of the parallel-transfers, participants were able to pick up full names and addresses of their separate-selves. Often they tapped in on experiences which transpired ten, twenty or thirty years ago. "I saw myself as a woman working at a desk in an accounting office. The desk calendar said, 'October 3, 1956,'" would be a typical response. Only a few have gone to the trouble of following up on this information and some of these have not checked out, while others have been correct in some details.

On a few occasions the verifications have been quick and easy; others have taken considerable detective work. In Portland, Oregon, we conducted the parallel-search in the morning sessions, and Cherry Hartman, a psychiatric social worker for Lutheran Family Services, received answers to all of the questions I'd asked of the hypnotized subjects. Instead of sharing lunch with the group, she found a telephone and attempted to follow up on the input via long distance. At the beginning of the afternoon session, she shared this information with the ninety other participants:

"In the parallel-life transfer, I went into a lifetime as James Arthur Phelps. I was an encyclopedia salesman and the year was 1963. The address I got was (full street address, city and state). My wife's name was Jackie. I checked this out with the help of a long distance operator and found the address to be real, but there is no one by that name living there now. I was able to talk to a woman who lives a few houses away and she told me that a Phelps family had lived on the block ten years ago . . . Also she verified the wife's name."

In conducting the group parallel-lives search, after hypnosis is induced, I provide instructions quite similar to those used with Calinda in the previous chapter. Prior to the actual transference, the group is instructed to experience only neutral, positive or happy situations as their own separate-self. Some of the basic questions, which I often vary, are: "What is the situation you now find yourself within? Your name, address or identifying landmarks? The date? Your career, or impressions as to how you primarily spend your time? Your hobbies?

An important situation? etc." When the group awakens, I ask those willing to share the information to come to the stage and relate their impressions into the microphone. The following are actual and typical examples of the responses:

Female participant, age 28: I went back, or went over and found myself in the year 1965. My name is Johanna Harris and I live in Peru. I'm a nurse, and the only way you can get to where I am is on the river boat that brings supplies, which we get once a month. The village that I live in—there's two very large huts . . . grass type huts and there's four or five smaller ones for the individual people. My hobbies are the children of the village and they're very small. I also go hunting for rocks and gems, getting off in the jungle by myself. This might also explain why my back hurts sometimes. I happen to be handling people in the hospital that can't do for themselves. They can't move themselves, and the chief of the village especially . . . he's a very large man and he's very heavy to try to move. This parallel experience came in much more vividly than any of the past life regressions which I've received thus far in the seminar.

Female participant, age 40: When the impressions started to come in, I saw myself with a cup of coffee in my hand . . . and I was in a submarine . . . it was very stuffy and it was 1943. I don't know what I was doing, but I saw this and then your voice came in and you told us to move to a happy time in our lives and I was with my wife, name Hilda, and we were on a picnic. There were some children playing there with us. You asked what my name was and it was Jon . . . and the last name I got was Bloomstone. That doesn't sound like a German name. I knew I was German. We lived in Heidelberg at 14 Steppguard (phonetic spelling). When you asked about one of the most important people to me, I seemed to go backward to my childhood, seeing myself at six and I was living in Switzerland,

and my mother was the most important person to me, and my father was some kind of scholar. One of your last questions triggered the submarine again and I was back in 1943, and I was a reader of some kind, working with maps and charts.

Female participant, age 39: I kept fighting going completely "out" during the session. I got very brief information, but . . . (she is crying and has a hard time speaking) . . . I first picked up on her in 1947 at the age of nine. She was born approximately nine months after I was in the same town, Philadelphia . . . the same hospital and her name was Susan. She was living in Detroit at the age of nine, around the Lake Michigan area. Then this other information started coming in. It was a real shocker . . . in 1962. She lost a child that I birthed in December of '62. There is other cross-tie information here that I can't relate to the group (crying more). In 1975, Susan was involved in a sailing accident that crippled her and eventually led to her death in October of last year. Well, I know that all of this has had a lot to do with all that has happened to me in this year . . . I got this out of it. I can describe the house she lived in. It was frame, one story with a basement—very Victorian style . . . and white with blue trim on the outside.

Male participant, age 48: If I can accept this, I am also a doctor or was a doctor in 1969, practicing in New York City. I couldn't get his name, but I guarantee you I'd recognize his offices if I were to ever see them. I saw the office door with many names on it, but they were fuzzy. Anyway, I'm probably in my late fifties or early sixties and have three grown children. My wife died several years ago, and I'm now living alone in an apartment in Manhattan. An interesting fact here is that in my own reality, I was a medic in Korea, I was good at it and learned quickly, but saw enough of human suffering to last me a lifetime. After the war, I started my own manufacturing business instead of pursuing medicine . . . at least this part of me did.

Another time a male participant, about 30, received strong impressions of being a very pretty young woman in France. He received enough information to probably find her and was talking about the idea of taking his vacation in that country to see if he could. We all asked that if he found himself in the position of making love to himself, he would let us know what the experience was like.

On several occasions, the situations have been extremely unusual and are hard to relate to the present life. Cherry Overton is the twenty-seven-year-old owner of the Book 'N Browse bookstore in Dallas, Texas. The following is her parallel-transfer experience in the Dallas seminar: "It was as if I was pulled into another world. It was a capsule . . . a city capsule, and I was drawn to a woman named Cloris. First I was looking through the glass and she said, 'Come on in . . . Hi, how are you?' Then I was inside and she continued talking to me. 'You're doing a good job and I really like you. I'm glad that you are on my team. Just keep it up because the better you do, the better I do.'

"I said, 'Yeah, well, thanks.'

"I was just sitting there talking to her and it was really neat. But your words and instructions, Dick, were really interrupting what was happening. Anyway, she was older at first; then she went back in time to show me what she looked like when she was younger . . . about my age now. She told me, 'You can come up and talk with me anytime; we are one and the same.'

"This whole thing is incredible!" Cherry said, shaking her head. "Anyway, as I was first being pulled in, I thought that the city looked a bit crowded; but when I was inside and walking around, it was very spacious, very open and clean. There was a lot of greenery. Cloris explained to me that her job was monitoring people like me and people like you. She drew me to her psychically, but she also has this machinery she works with. She also explained that they love nature and live out here in nature, and their religion is nature. She has a husband and a son, and said, 'We are all part of you.' After a while, she told me, 'Why don't you run on now. You know you can come back up here now that you know your way. You'll come back and visit me again.' I said, 'OK,' and I really hated to leave."

Upon listening to the master tape of the entire afternoon sessions, I realized that I had not instructed the group to explore a parallel on the earth plane of existence, so I don't know where Cherry may have gone—another here-and-now reality existing in an alternate frequency . . . another planet or an orbiting space city? All might be potentials.

In a search of old and new metaphysical books we could find references to the "constant now" idea of no-time, but only vague passages which might allude to simultaneous multiple incarnations. As I said in the beginning of the book, when it is time for new understanding to be released from the nonphysical realms, I believe it is channeled through many people at the same time. It was welcome substantiation to read *Psychic Politics,* the new aspect psychology book by Jane Roberts, published in the fall of 1976. In it Jane relates information channeled through Seth: "He said, 'You can live more than one life in one time. You are neurologically turned in to one particular field of actuality that you recognize.' "

Seth: If you could think of a multidimensional body existing at one time in different realities, and appearing differently within those realities, then you could get a glimpse of what is involved.

Seth: You live more than one life at a time. You do not experience your century simply from one separate vantage point, and the individuals alive in any given century have far deeper connections than you realize. You do not experience your space-time world, then, from one but from many viewpoints.

Dr. Gil E. Gilly is a fine telepathic psychic with a

65

national reputation. Over lunch I asked him, "In doing individual psychic readings for people, have you ever come across situations in which an individual's present personal problems are actually emanating from a parallel-self—someone else they are spiritually connected to who is also alive on the earth at this time?"

"All of the time!" was Gil's answer. "Simultaneous multiple incarnations are a reality, but your other-selves cannot affect you unless you allow them to."

Thea Alexander is the author of *2150 A.D.*, a novel about reincarnation which was originally published privately in 1971. The book became an underground metaphysical best seller and was recently rewritten and published by a large publishing company. In the rewrite, she included the concept of simultaneous multiple incarnations. I asked Thea, who is an old friend, what prompted this addition to the story.

"I've come to understand through my own awareness that this concept is valid," she replied. "We all exist as part of a soul matrix, exploring numerous potentials in the constant 'now.' As we evolve in our acceptance of what is as perfect . . . not only perfect, but joyously perfect . . . we grow in awareness, we permit barriers to fall away. The only thing that prevents us from being totally aware of all our existences is our narrow perspective, our fears. When we outgrow these fears, the barriers drop, our blinders fall off and we see the total self—not just the self limited to this small portion of time and space. We can then, at our option, focus on any level—past, present, or future, and merge them, taking the seeds of awareness from any of our separate selves, to accelerate evolution of the others."

Thea's words are stimulating; unfortunately, there is no way to "absolutely prove" parallel-selves are a reality, any more than we can prove the concept of reincarnation is valid. Yet, the evidence is certainly "interesting," and I know that there are research areas we have not examined. Hopefully another year will provide much additional information.

CHAPTER 7

CASE HISTORY:
A METAPHYSICAL
EXAMINATION

Owen Warner is a personal friend who once sat in on one of my lectures and a group regression. He'd received vivid impressions of a prior life in ancient Greece, but the entire subject of reincarnation was of little interest to him. Our friendship was really based on a mutual interest in exploring the Arizona back country in our four-wheel-drive pickup trucks. Over the past few years we've experienced many fun, hair-raising times racing down shallow river beds, up and over sand dunes, and side-hilling forty-five-degree cliffs. Both Trenna and Owen's wife, Gail, usually came along on our safaris. Although they would often spend a good part of the day with knuckles white from clutching the dashboards and doorframes, both were good sports and did little complaining.

Early in 1977 I heard that the Warners were separated and contemplating divorce. The news made me very sad and I called Owen at his printing company office to ask him to have lunch with me. "He hasn't worked here for two weeks," the receptionist said. I tried to call Gail, but there was no answer at their house. It was another week before a mutual friend informed me that Gail had gone to stay with her parents in California and Owen, being unwilling to stay in their home alone, had taken a room in a cheap motel on the Phoenix–Van Buren strip. Such places do not usually have room phones so I decided to drive over and find him if possible.

The Siesta Paradise Motel is typical of a hundred others in the valley; postwar, slump block construction with dry rot slowly devouring the exposed wood portions of the buildings. A "Rooms—Day—Week—Month" sign beckoned at the entrance. The typical landscaping of oleanders and palm trees was overgrown, but graciously helped to hide the dilapidated state of repairs.

Owen was sitting alone by the pool in cut-offs, a beer can in his lap and a partially consumed six-pack on the table beside him. He saw me approaching and casually tossed a Coors across the pool in my direction. "Hello, good buddy . . . welcome to paradise."

I sat down in the chair beside him, popping the top of the almost warm beer. Half of it exploded. "Paradise, huh?" I was looking at the underchlorinated pool. Both the green and black plague had set in. "If you climb into that I think it would eat you, Owen."

"I may be dumb, Richard, but I'm not crazy. There was a lady who looked like a prune out here earlier. She was making noises about going swimming and I haven't seen her since, so it must have gotten her. Maybe that would be the easy way out?"

"Is that self-pity or warm Coors talking?" I asked, looking around at the junglelike environment. "I'm between seminar tours, and for once there is no writing or recording deadline hanging over my head. How about running up to Coyote Springs with me? I'll drive and we can talk."

It took about an hour to get to the springs area below Four Peaks, a landmark cluster of mountains northeast of Scottsdale. There was little communication en route. Owen climbed out of the cab to open the Forest Service wire gate that led to the four-wheel trail back to the creek. "Thanks for getting me out of paradise," he said as he climbed back in. "I feel better already."

Although only a few minutes above the saguaro-covered desert, Coyote Springs is literally a forest of cottonwood and hardwood trees, following along a creek now swollen by the melting snow from the peaks above.

"Want me to talk?" Owen said, sitting cross legged on a large rock in the middle of the creek.

"Not unless you want to," I replied. "Just wanted to make sure you were still alive."

"Everybody we know really thinks I'm off the wall, Dick. I guess I am. I've become some kind of weirdo according to Gail. Her parents think I'm nuts. My parents think I'm a nut." He was staring down at the water, stirring it with a stick as he talked.

"Let 'em," I responded.

"I'm not looking for anybody to take my side, really," he said, now looking directly at me.

"Owen, I don't take sides. I guess you don't know enough about that side of me, my work or my philosophy to know that, but I guarantee you there is no way I'd take your side or Gail's side. To judge anyone else is stupid and absolutely impossible from my perspective, no matter what they've done. There are simply too many unseen influences that can be affecting everyone involved."

"What do you mean, unseen influences?" he asked, holding a beer can in the air as if offering a toast. "When I think about it. I think maybe I was just looking for this kind of trouble. I've messed up my marriage by messing around with about six different lovely ladies. That also meant losing my kid. I screwed up at work because my marriage became such a scene I couldn't concentrate on what I was supposed to be doing. I have a stack of unopened bills that I don't believe. Now I'm drinking too so I don't have to think about any of it."

It was hard for him to get the talk started, and he was now back to staring at the creek again. I'd known Owen and Gail for about three years. He was a dark-complected, husky man of thirty, whose outdoorsy looks seemed out of place in a business suit. We'd occasionally have lunch together and his weekday appearance always jolted me. "I don't like it either," he explained, "but you don't walk into some advertising executive's office in boots and Levi's and expect to get the job. You have to be an author and weirdo hypnotist to get away with things like that."

A few months ago he'd been a happily married man with a beautiful wife and seven-year-old son, the star of the local Little League. As a printing salesman consultant he serviced many high commission accounts in Arizona and California. The family lived in a comfortable Scottsdale neighborhood, and Gail spent most of her time at home. Philosophically neither Owen or Gail had any particular beliefs or religious backgrounds.

"Unseen influences are any forces that are affecting you without you consciously realizing it," I explained. "Much of this isn't part of your belief, but you are familiar with mental and physical problems. I believe that there are also other factors such as *astrology, biorhythms, parallel-selves, past life relationships with those you know today, discarnate entities, incompatible frequency possibilities, brain wave similarities, numerous forms of psychic attack and positive and negative ions . . .* just to name a few."

"Most of that is Greek to me," Owen responded. "It also sounds very dramatic. I read your last book about past lives and being born to be together, so I know some of what you're talking about. Gail and I thought we were a perfect example of your hypothesis. I guess that wasn't the case."

"Owen, I guarantee that you and Gail were born again to be together or you certainly wouldn't be going through what you are now experiencing. The basic fact that you were married says it to me, but when there is much joy or pain in a relationship it is a karmic situation and will usually be filled with tests and opportunities. There have only been a couple of marital relationships in which I've been unable to find past life ties. In both cases they were machine-like associations, seemingly devoid of emotions."

Owen continued to explain his situation in more

detail and I will capsulize it to save space. The Warners had shared a fine marriage for nearly eight years. During that time he'd had a couple of "one night flings that didn't amount to anything," but basically he and Gail shared a good sexual relationship. Then he met a girl, a receptionist, and they had lunch together. There was an instant rapport and within the week they were meeting for lunch and love-making at her apartment. "That incident seemed to open the floodgates," he said. "I just started making it with every pretty lady I could get into bed. At first it was just the excitement and the fun of it all. It wasn't that I didn't love Gail, it was just that our relationship had become routine. I certainly never intended to hurt her, or for her to find out about it."

What followed were the complications of involvement. Over the next few months Owen began to "wear down" mentally. Out of subconscious anxiety, guilt or fear, he began to self-destruct his home environment.

"There were horrible scenes," he said. "I'd promise Gail I wouldn't see any other women. I'd really mean it at the time, yet I'd always do it again. There were many other factors. We were at each other about everything. I seemed to be pulled in every direction at the same time. I'd argue that I wanted Gail to stay with me and make it work, and yet at the same time I'd start a fight or do something that pushed her away all the faster. Then she started doing the same thing. It was like two crazy people each trying to stick our fingers in a hole in a dike to save it, while with our other hands we were digging brand new holes."

We were now returning to Scottsdale. I turned off the Beeline Highway and on to Shea Blvd. "You really think you're the only one who has ever been through the relationship crazies?" I asked.

"Feels that way," he responded.

"I've been there, Owen. Believe me, I know, and so do millions and millions of others. I used an introductory poem in one of my poetry books that really sums it up."

71

No matter what you've
experienced . . .

the highs
and
the lows—

the joy
and
the pain—

You are not alone—

So many others have
been there

So many are there
right now.

I had Owen write his problems on a piece of paper.
We then set a date for some individual regression
work and I asked him to look up his exact birth time
so an astrologer could examine him from afar.

That night I explained the situation very briefly
to Trenna and asked her if she'd be willing to work on
it. She agreed. Through the years of working with
hypnotic techniques she has developed some unique
abilities that have now been demonstrated in front of
thousands of people in our seminars. One of the most
dramatic demonstrations is a chakra hook-up. In this
case a volunteer is chosen from the participants.
Trenna lies down on a bed while the subject sits behind her in a chair. I then hypnotise Trenna and complete an elaborate set of instructions which connect
the top three energy chakras of the two people. A
very real "psychic link" is now established. After the
trance is deepened, she is instructed to draw upon
the connecting link and allow the memories from the
subconscious mind of the volunteer to flow into her
own mind. She is instructed to relive a portion of a
past life that would be of value for the volunteer

subject to know about in the present. In 1976 we did some touring with a friend, author and fellow researcher, Brad Steiger. The following examples of Trenna's abilities were included in Brad's book, *You Will Live Again*.

Los Angeles: The volunteer was a woman of approximately thirty. Trenna was speaking in the voice of a small child of seven or eight. She was listening to a big fight between her parents, and found out that her daddy was not her real father. Mother had been pregnant by someone else at the time of the marriage. After this the father left and never returned. When Trenna was moved out of the past and into the Higher-Self, she explained many things about the present life and its relationship to other times.

Once I had awakened Trenna I asked the volunteer if any of it made any sense. "Everything she said . . . everything she said that I know about," she explained. "I've had a recurring nightmare all of my life. It's always the same. My father, in my present life, is not really my father. I've had it ever since I was a little girl and it has haunted me." She now started to cry.

San Francisco: The volunteer was a woman of approximately thirty-five. Trenna was speaking in a fearful voice about hiding in the cellar with her eighteen-year-old sister. She was sixteen. Upstairs they could hear German soldiers searching the house. The soldiers found the girls and started to carry the sister off to another room. The sixteen-year-old began to scream and wouldn't stop, which angered one of the men to the degree that he grabbed her and strangled her to death. Trenna also related much accurate contemporary information about the woman's life.

Even before awakening Trenna, the volunteer was shaking and crying, just listening to Trenna relate the situation. When I asked her about it, she completely broke down. "Oh my God," she sobbed. "All of my life if anyone so much as even touches my neck I become hysterical and it takes me hours to calm down.

73

I know that is what happened . . . I could see it transpiring while she talked. Everything she said about my current life is absolutely accurate, even down to the young, black-haired boy in my life."

Dallas, Texas: The volunteer was a man of approximately forty. Trenna was telling of a sea captain lifetime and an event that transpired in 1897. The captain had eliminated half of the necessary lifeboats to provide more cargo-carrying space. There was an explosion on board the ship, and when the ship started to sink he was the first to make a space for himself while half his men drowned. During the night he threw a wounded man out of the lifeboat to conserve water. Those who remained in the boat eventually threw him overboard. From the Higher-Self, Trenna explained that all of his present life he has had a paranoid fear of taking any form of responsibility, and that he continued to punish himself for something that happened in the past. "You have constant deep depressions, and your stomach becomes a spasmodic knot under tension," she said. "It all relates to this past life and it is time you let go of the guilt. Let go of it now. Use your time in this life to help others. Only you can erase this karma, by believing you can."

"I believe she touched something, didn't she, sir," I said, looking at the now white-faced volunteer.

"Everything! Even down to the knot she talked about. I began to have the stomach spasms in the middle of the regression. Yes, I've spent my life hiding from any form of responsibility. Yes, the up and down depressions have bothered me all of my life." He buried his face in his hands, explaining that he couldn't talk about it for awhile.

In addition to these public demonstrations we found that Trenna could hold a letter from someone who is troubled and with the same hypnotic techniques form a long-distance link through which she has accurately described the past lives and present-day effects of the writer. That was the technique to be used this evening.

"In Owen's case let's not look for anything specific, such as past or parallel-lives. Not in the beginning," Trenna said, getting comfortable in the recliner. "I think we'd be better off to simply attempt to open a psychic channel and see what comes through. If nothing much is happening, then you can begin to direct it."

I agreed. Trenna now held Owen's ring in one hand and his writings about his problems in the other. I induced a deep trance and completed the chakra hook-up instructions. "All right, the connection is now complete and I want you to speak up and tell me anything that might be of value in understanding the present-day effects in Owen's life."

Several minutes passed in silence before Trenna spoke in a faraway voice: "Owen is an empath, thus he is being subjected to mental input that he mistakenly believes to be his own. He does not know this. A very tall, dark-haired woman is a strong influence here. There is much more, but it is best that the revelations come through Owen's own experiences if you expect acceptance. He should have a complete physical examination."

That was the complete session. The next day I talked to Owen and asked him several questions: "Do you know what an empath is, Owen?"

"No."

"It is an individual who is very sensitive to the thoughts of others, or to psychic input. Do you ever know what someone is going to say before they say it?"

"Oh sure, all the time. It became a joke with Gail and me, but that's just because we lived together for so long. I knew her and got so I could predict her words."

"O.K., did she do the same with you?"

"Once in awhile I suppose, but not often."

"When Gail was depressed, or when you are around anyone who is depressed, how do you handle it?"

"God, I usually catch it, Dick. I got so I could spot

it ahead of time with Gail, so I'd just take Bobby and we'd go play ball. If I didn't, I'd get just as depressed as she was. Gail isn't a depressed sort of person, though. Usually it was just once a month when she had her period."

"One more question. Do you know a very tall dark-haired girl who is important to you in any way?"

"Sure, Alison. The lovely that I was telling you about that works as a receptionist. The one all this got started with."

"What is the situation with Alison today?"

"She'd like to be very involved. I see her once in awhile, but that's it."

"All right, I'll talk to you soon, but do me and yourself one favor. Get a good physical checkup and tell the doctor about your present situation."

Assumption: When Owen met Alison they were very attracted to each other on the surface. Assuming that Owen is psychically sensitive (an empath) he could have been very influenced by her thoughts and desires as well.

Everyone has a medically measurable brain wave, and tests have proven that two people who have close brain waves, or exactly the same brain waves, will experience a higher degree of ESP with each other than with others. The average wave is Alpha 6. If, for example, Owen and Alison both share an Alpha 6, then with Owen's empathic receiving abilities, Alison is projecting directly into his mind with tremendous effectiveness. Because they are sexually involved there is additional unseen power influencing the relationship.

From a metaphysical perspective it is through the balanced sexual polarity of a man and woman that we recharge the life energies. Ideally the experience is multilevel, establishing a mental/physical union resulting in a harmonious unity. Sex, of course, is a powerful force and relates beyond the physical. It can easily create mental, emotional and psychic links; and the psychic and probably karmic aspects do not disappear when the physical union has discontinued.

Owen said that Alison was the beginning of his involvement with several different women. As an example of a probability: Alison is a highly sexual person and could have been transmitting her own sexual desires and fantasies to Owen. If she was fantasizing having sex with him while masturbating, although he was miles away, he could have mentally picked up sexual desires that he perceived to be his own. The result was additional extramarital involvement.

A few days later Owen called to tell me about the results of his physical examination. He had a mild case of hypoglycemia, which as an abnormally low level of glucose in the blood. The doctor had put him on a high protein diet.

Assumption: Hypoglycemia is a body imbalance that often causes irrational behavior. The disease alone may have been responsible for many of Owen's actions and reactions over the past few months. It also may have weakened his normal defenses against external influences from sources like Alison, or even from discarnate entities on the other side.

Trenna used her hypnotic trance abilities again in an attempt to establish if discarnates or lower astral plane entities were involved: "Owen is in a low state," she began. "He is down mentally and physically. His present alcohol intake worsens the condition. Just as anyone in a similar situation would be, he is surrounded by lower astral discarnates and their presence is a negative influence. Yet I perceive no particular malevolence or plan in this situation. His present level of awareness is simply attracting these confused beings who act as unseen leeches attempting to suck energy. Once a degree of harmony is restored and his own aura strengthened they will be unable to influence him."

Owen had provided me with his birth data and I'd turned it over to a fine professional astrologer, asking her to do a complete examination of the last few months. She reported that Owen was going through his primary Saturn transet, just as most people do around his age. This usually turns the individual's life upside down for several months. In some cases the upheaval is channeled in positive directions, in others, such as Owen's, it takes more destructive forms.

Assumption: The astrological influences were simply fuel added to an unseen, yet uncontrolled fire that was raging behind the scenes of Owen's life. The movement of the stars wasn't causing the problems, but they were influencing them.

I often quote Hazel Mooney in an attempt to explain astrological influences. Hazel is one of the finest and most responsible astrologers I've worked with. She usually does her charts on tape, and before the reading begins, she makes the following statement:

"The ultimate purpose of astrology is to serve as a guide through your physical life, but the soul must have awakened before the value of the horoscope can be fully appreciated. Self understanding and destiny— the self must be known, the destiny must be fulfilled: therefore, character is destiny. The birth chart is merely a symbolic representation of potential development. All of the aspects are intended only for learning and are, therefore, benevolent. Since all suffering is the result of ignorance, astrology seeks to answer the question 'Why.' It is a benefit, therefore, to know both the harmonious and inharmonious aspects in your chart. All fate is the result of thoughts which are the roots of your character. To know yourself is to become wise and thus to master fate. Free will is a divine gift to all. As you gain in understanding, you can avoid much of the negative conditioning and use the positive aspects to full enjoyment. The desire to give love and be loved will reach a perfected state in you through many lifetimes of practicing, giving and understanding love. So continue to unfold in love, believe in love and give of the inner self to love. Eventually you will reach that level where all is expressed and experienced in fullness. If others do not understand your

giving warm love to life, and do not return it to you
pay it no heed, for it does not matter to your own
inner awareness. You are reaching for the ultimate,
and you have to experience many, many lives before
it is finally attained."

A week had passed since Owen and I first talked
at Coyote Springs. Without doing past and parallel-
life searches, we already had considerable data and
knowledge as a basis to begin to work with. Yet before
I explained any of it to Owen I wanted to complete
some basic hypnotic sessions.

He arrived at our home in much better spirits than
when I'd seen him last. "Maybe it's just the high
protein diet, but I really feel like a new man . . . or at
least like a lot of weight has been lifted off the old
one. Doc said, 'Little or no booze,' so I'm making it
with a couple of 'light' beers a day."

We all talked about general things for awhile, then
I asked him if he was ready to go to work.

"You mean go to sleep?" he laughed. "Sure, when I
sat in on that seminar group session you did, I
thought I'd been taken on a silent movie peyote trip.
This time I take it I'll be asked to speak up and answer questions?"

"Right. Now settle into that chair. Trenna is going
to sit right behind me and attempt to psychically tap
in on everything you are experiencing. She'll go into
a light trance, but will still be able to write me notes
if it is of value to the session."

OWEN
First Session

Hypnosis induced and regression preparation completed. The following instructions were then given.
"You are going to go back into a previous lifetime in
which you and your present wife Gail were together
before, if indeed the two of you have shared experi-

79

ences in previous times. If you have been together in many incarnations, I want your subconscious mind to choose the lifetime that would be of primary value to examine at this time. A life that will help us to understand the present situation and the underlying causes. I will count backwards from five to one. On the count of one you will see yourself in a very important or clarifying situation." (Instructions completed.)

Q. Speak up and tell me what you see and what is happening at this time.

A. What do you want? . . . I'm in the middle of a party meeting!

Q. I apologize for interrupting you, but can you tell me your name?

A. Luther Roderk! (His voice was stern and irritated.)

Q. What party meeting are you attending?

A. Centrists, of course.

Q. And what country are you living in?

A. Germany.

Q. Can you tell me the year?

A. You're not too well informed are you, sir? It is 1912. We are well behind the Socialists and I have considerable work to do.

Q. All right, I want you to let go of this and move to something that will happen in the future. It will be an important situation. (Instructions given.) What do you perceive at this time, Luther?

A. Ida is in the garden with the children, I'm watching them from the upstairs bedroom window. They are very happy.

Q. Your voice sounds sad. Is there anything wrong?

A. We fought for many hours last night. Ida becomes more involved with the children every day . . . and less involved with me. She says I think of nothing but politics and am a bad father. She has to provide the love for both of us to the three children. I don't believe the situation is that severe. I pay as much attention as any man to his children, or nearly as much. She uses the children as a rationale to avoid attending party functions with me. She hates politics.

Additional questioning at this time simply provided a broader picture of a relationship in which the wife was withdrawing from her husband because of his career. He responded by becoming more involved than ever in the political activities of the day. Ida and Luther remained together and from external appearances shared a fine marriage. Privately it became an arrangement for the sake of the children.

Assumption: Owen was still carrying subconscious hostilities towards Gail (who was Ida) because of her rejection of him in the past life. His involvement with other women in the present was a way to strike back at her. Consciously of course he did not want to hurt her, but there were subconscious forces at work that had set into motion in Germany at the turn of the century.

Owen was still in deep hypnosis and I decided to maneuver the questioning in a new direction. "I now want you to let go of this and I want you to move backward in time once again. If there is another lifetime in which Owen and Gail, Luther and Ida, have been together, and if it will help to explain the circumstances of the German incarnations, I want you to move back to that previous time and place . . . to an important situation." (Instructions given.)

Q. What do you perceive at this time?
A. I'm standing in the colonnade waiting for my friend, Medson. He will be here soon.
Q. Where are you now? Can you tell me the name of this place?
A. Seleucia.
Q. Is that a country?

A. Seleucia is the most beautiful city in all Greece ... the flower of the Hellenistic world. (He speaks in a superior tone with a slightly effeminate feeling. I can't help but smile, for Owen himself is somewhat of a redneck by contemporary standards.) Trenna, who has remained in a light trance up until now, hunches over in a pained manner and scrawls something on the notepad in her lap: "Extremely violent situation ... knife ... death."

Q. What is your name?

A. Carneades, first son of Serasis.

Q. What is happening now, Carneades?

A. Medson is coming now ... but he's yelling at those men. Everyone is mad. These philosophical wars in the forum get out of hand. Ridiculous! Oh no ... no ... NO ... he stabbed Medson ... HE STABBED MEDSON!!!! (Owen begins to scream and thrash in the chair so he is immediately removed from the mental environment he is reliving. Once quieted, I move him up into the Higher-Self realms of his mind and from this level continue to question.)

Q. You will now remember both of the past lives you have just reexamined, but you will remember objectively, without pain or emotion. Let the understanding come in, and on the count of three you will be aware of all that has transpired. 1, 2, 3. (Owen jerked, took a deep breath and was quiet.) From this perspective you have all of the knowledge of all of your former lifetimes right there at your mental fingertips. I now want to know how the lifetime in ancient Greece relates to your life as Owen Warner.

A. (Two or three minutes passed before Owen spoke.) Now I understand. Gail was Medson. We were friends in that lifetime.

Assumption: Gail had been murdered in Greece because of a difference of opinion in philosophical ideas, thus she carried a subconscious fear of political involvement forward into the German lifetime as Ida. Perhaps any activity which involved conflicting ideologies would have triggered a similar reaction. She lost Owen as a friend in ancient Greece, and feared losing him as a husband in Germany. Owen in turn looked upon her actions in Germany as rejection.

Like the ripples from a stone tossed in a lake, the causes and effects of actions and reactions ripple through time. I decided to awaken Owen, but since he did not understand reincarnation or metaphysical concepts, I decided to block his memories of the past lives for awhile. He was a somnambulistic subject and this was easily accomplished with a simple suggestion.

(End of first session.)

"How are you feeling?" I asked.

"Great, but nothing happened, did it?" he responded, rubbing his eyes.

"Oh yes, plenty happened and we have it all professionally recorded here on tape. But for right now I'd prefer to gather more data before we talk about it all. There are a couple of things that I do need to know and I want you to answer me truthfully, ok?"

"Sure."

"Have you ever studied German history, about the turn of this century, or ancient Greek history?"

"Not that I know of. Maybe in high school, but if so I don't recall it. I had two years at ASU, but I know I didn't take it there. Is that where I went back to?"

We decided to do another session the following day. This time I hoped to seek out any knowledge of parallel-selves that might be subconsciously or superconsciously influencing the situation. After three unsuccessful attempts at establishing a transference, I gave up. "You either don't have any counterparts, or you're unwilling to admit to it, even in a deep trance."

"I don't know what the hell you're talking about,"

83

Owen stated from his relaxed position in the hypnosis recliner.

"I'm glad you don't have any," I told him. "I'd hate to have to explain it all to you later. Let's try something else."

OWEN
Second Session

Hypnosis induced and regression preparation completed. The following instructions were then given: "If you have ever known the woman you now know as Alison in a previous lifetime, I want you to go back to an important situation that transpired between you. If you've known each other in more than one life, your subconscious mind will choose the life that would be of the most value to examine at this time." (Instructions given.) "Speak up now and tell me what you see and what you are doing."

A. I seem to be hurt . . . someone is helping me . . . she is trying to get me up on my feet. Very dizzy . . . can't seem to . . . fell down again. (As opposed to reliving this situation as Owen had done with the two previous lifetimes, he seemed to be watching this one from a detached perspective.)

Q. Tell me more about what is happening.

A. Very dark-skinned people . . . not blacks . . . Indians I believe . . . some kind of Indians in a semi-tropical environment. I'm now lying on a mat, she is taking care of me . . . feeding me. The walls of the structure look like white plaster . . . maybe plaster over stone. The roof is thatched . . . it's raining . . . yes, raining. Some rain is coming through the roof.

Q. Let's move forward in time a few days, on the count of three you'll be there: 1, 2, 3. What is happening now?

A. Oh-h-h-h-h. . . . She is loving me. (Owen's body

begins to move rhythmically in the chair. I moved him forward in time again one month.)

Q. What is happening now?

A. I don't see anything.

Q. All right, let's go backwards in time to the last situation you recall. On the count of one you'll be there: 3, 2, 1.

A. I'm still on the mat . . . just looking up at the roof . . . but I seem to be floating . . . just floating up . . . and around . . . I can see myself lying there with my eyes open watching me float up here.

Q. I believe you have left your body. Are you dead?

A. I don't think so . . . ah . . . she is screaming that I'm dead . . . but if I am, I'm still here . . . just floating around.

Q. Someone will soon come by to communicate with you.

A. I'll just be floating.

(End of second session.)

Once again I blocked the memories of the session from Owen's conscious mind, and upon awakening him I explained that the next session would be to teach him some techniques that would be good to incorporate into his life. I also asked that he define his desires, writing them out as simply as possible on paper. "What do you want to happen in the next few months, Owen? Spell it out."

Historic Follow-up: All of the historic facts that could be checked were verified. *Germany:* The Centrists were the second most popular of five primary political parties in Germany in 1912. The Socialists held 110 seats to the Centrists' 90. *Greece:* Seleucia was a major Hellenistic city, ranking with Alexandria and Antioch. A gridiron architectural plan was used in these cities, with the focal point being the marketplace and forum. Facing this square were shops and offices fronted by a colonnade. Philosophy was extremely important to the Greeks at this time.

At our next meeting I explained to Owen how the thoughts of others could be affecting him. Thought projection affects everyone, but when directed towards someone with a psychic sensitivity, or empathic abilities, the effects can be very strong. I told him about several of the case histories in our own files. None of the individuals were empaths, yet their personal lives were being upset by telepathic projections.

Case A: An ex-husband was purposely using mental techniques, learned through his involvement with one of the country's foremost awareness-expanding organizations, to psychically attack his former wife. He had not wanted the divorce and once the marriage was formally dissolved, he told her that he would destroy her. The techniques could be called by many names, but they all amount to "black magic." Within a couple of months the woman was unable to eat, to concentrate on her job, and was experiencing physical pains. One of California's finest medical clinics and a top psychologist gave her every conceivable test, and uncovered nothing. Yet the conditions became worse and worse, until after reading my book, she called me. I had some available time, so she came to Arizona and we used regressive hypnosis to find a lineage of negative lifetimes with her ex. What she needed was spiritual protection techniques, and once they were instituted into her daily routine, all adverse effects dissipated and have not returned.

Case B: A young man of thirty-three worked in a large architectural firm as part of a bull-pen team of a dozen young architects. He was far more creative than the others, and at the first opportunity, management promoted him to new responsibilities and his own office. Shortly after the promotion he became very prone to depressions and his work began to suffer. Psychic investigation showed that the concentrated jealous thoughts of the other architects were affecting him. We taught him psychic shielding techniques and the depressions immediately alleviated.

Cases C, D, & E: All cases of a devoutly religious

86

family member, usually of a fundamentalist Christian sect, praying to change the direction of someone they love. In one case it was a mother trying to stop her son from marrying a woman she thought was evil. In another a mother did not want her daughter to be interested in metaphysical and psychic concepts. The third involved a boyfriend attempting to manipulate his girl into accepting his religion. In each case they spent hours praying for the deliverance of the ones they loved, and all of these concentrated thought forms, directed at the unknowing parties, were having disastrous effects: confusion, hysteria, and in one situation it nearly caused a complete mental breakdown. The perpetrators meant well, yet they unknowingly were using telepathic techniques to manipulate and control others, which is always wrong. In each case psychic blocking and protectory techniques eliminated the effects. Assertiveness training was also advised to teach kind, but firm, techniques to handle the religious loved ones.

I taught Owen how to use self-hypnosis (in the back of this book) and protection techniques. "You can use them with hypnosis, with meditation, or they can stand on their own. But do use them daily for awhile, always if you feel depressed in any way."

He agreed to try what I asked, but I felt as much to humor me as for any thought of self-improvement.

"O.K., show me the paper you wrote, Owen. The one about your desires and goals."

"How do you know I did it?" He smiled, reaching into his pocket. The words were printed very neatly on a piece of white typewriter paper: *I would like my life back the way it was six months ago. I love my wife more than anyone in the world, and I realize the beauty we had.*

"If it does work out this way, you realize it will never be the way it was six months ago," I said. "You wouldn't want it to be, for you've learned and grown in those months . . . and that is the reason you're alive. Do you think you could talk Gail into coming back to meet with Trenna and you and me? There are many things I'd like to explain to you both, the reports, assumptions, and the tape recordings of your regression sessions."

"I'll sure try to talk her into it," he replied.

It took all Saturday morning for Trenna and I to communicate our information to the Warners. We went over the astrology chart and the psychic input, played Owen's regression tapes, and explained our assumptions. It wasn't a matter of trying to prove anything, but to provide a basic overview for understanding. Gail said very little in response. Owen seemed to become progressively more interested and his questions increased.

"Good God, Richard, if all of these unseen influences were affecting me it amounts to a total predestination package. We can blame everything on destiny and thus reject all self-responsibility."

"No way, Owen. You are totally responsible for absolutely everything that happens to you . . . from a karmic or subconscious perspective. *And you are in full control of your destiny, but only when you have control of yourself.* If your level awareness is high and you are experiencing true inner harmony, the unseen influences cannot possibly affect you to any real degree. As an example, heavy astrological influence might simply cause you to swim a little harder against the currents of life, but it would never pull you under."

"*When you are no longer affected by a problem, you no longer have the problem,*" Trenna laughed.

"I'm not sure I got that," Owen said.

"Oh, that is my favorite line," I said. "It is one of the ultimate metaphysical concepts, but it has caused me to be accused of advocating 'stoicism.' In other words I advocate self mental reprogramming to eliminate negative external effects. Let's say every morning Gail grouched at you at breakfast. *It isn't her grouchy words that are affecting you, it is what you THINK about her grouchy words that is affecting you.* Program yourself to be unaffected by her grouching and although she may continue her morning verbal attacks, you won't care. Externally the problem remains, but since you are not affected you don't have a problem."

"I don't grouch at breakfast," Gail said softly.

"No, she doesn't," Owen added, putting his arm around her.

"I'd sure like to see you two make it," I said.

"I don't know, Dick; there is a lot of thinking that needs to be done," Gail said, gathering her belongings to leave. "I don't know how to thank you and Trenna for everything you've done with Owen."

Four months have passed since that Saturday morning. Today Gail and Owen are still married and from all reports are doing fine. We've been too busy to accept their weekend four-wheeling invitations, but I'm in the process of creating the time for my own back-country reality.

CHAPTER 8

OTHER CONCEPTS
OF REINCARNATION

I have not gone into the theme of reincarnation in this book. It is well covered in *You Were Born Again to Be Together,* and so many other authors have explained it in detail in their own volumes. As I stated initially, I believe that the past, as we think of the past within a sequential time concept, is affecting the present. You can call this reincarnation and karma. The one thing I am not absolutely sure of is how reincarnation actually works, and this is after ten years of intensive study and full-time involvement with regressive hypnosis into prior incarnations. There are hundreds of esoteric organizations and millions of individuals who would tell you and me exactly how it works . . . and they would *know* they are right. The problem is, I don't know that they are right. It's a very real concern that I may have educated myself right out of the accepted belief system, just as I've seen many friends of orthodox religious beliefs who begin to investigate metaphysics and evolve beyond their accepted faiths.

We've already covered the concept of "no time" . . . that everything is happening right now. We've also gone into parallel-lives or simultaneous multiple incarnations in great detail. The concepts seem to have considerable credibility and obviously could all be correct at the same time.

In all of the five-day seminars that Trenna and I conduct, we use a hypnotic technique to progress the groups into a future lifetime. This is done on the fifth day, when the participants are extremely well conditioned and at least ninety percent of them have vivid experiences. They are able to retain and discuss the impressions of lifetimes that are transpiring, up to two thousand years from now. Of the several hundred people we have worked with in this area of exploration, I don't believe anyone has progressed beyond the year 4000.

The participants are instructed to allow their own superconscious mind to choose a lifetime that they will be living in the future on the earth plane of existence and are commanded to experience only positive, neutral or happy situations that will transpire during that life. Once they have completed the time transfer, many questions are asked.

On comparing the tape-recorded discussions of their experiences, we've found no contradictions at all, and many cross-verifications. If the concept of "no-time" is valid, then you are also already living lifetimes somewhere in the future . . . as we perceive the future. You are probably interacting with many of the same people who are important in your present life in the future as well as the past.

THE CREATOR CONCEPT
(Spiritual Genetic Lineage)

There is another concept which I touched on in the last book and would like to expand upon in this one. It was initially introduced through Wassily Kandinsky,* one of the discarnate identities who speaks through fine artist David Chethlahe Paladin. We call it "The Creator Concept" or "Spiritual Genetics."

---

* Kandinsky was the famous Russian artist who died in 1941.

This supposition would claim that you are who you are—you have never been anyone else and will never be anyone else; but when you die, your knowledge and energy will remain throughout eternity as you. From the nonphysical realms, you will then be free to explore new potentials. Thoughts are energy and they create; they are creating your life right now, and they will create your future. Let's say that you are now a woman and after you experience physical death in this life, you decide that you'd like to explore the potential of a man—a businessman in a large industrial center. You also decide that you'd like to be a farmer, in some small European community and let's say, a female dancer in the Orient.

So you now create these lives, these potentials of exploration, as extensions of yourself. Once anything is created, it is freed; so the three identities will be your creations, but free individuals. They will be on your frequency or your time/space lineage, so you will "feel" and experience through them . . . all their joys and misery, their successes and failures—their learning. Thus you will evolve through this expansion of experience. Intuitively all three of your creations will receive information from each other; and through a system of spiritual genetics, all would share the same past life lineage. In other words, if they were all to be hypnotically regressed in the future, they would experience a past life as you. You are their creator, and their karma would be to solve the things you hadn't learned in the physical. Of course, they would also be the beneficiary of all the positive or good karma you created during your physical life. All three would be parallel-selves or simultaneous multiple incarnations.

Once your three creations live out their lives and cross over to the nonphysical realms, they will be free to create and explore their own new potentials.

If you accept this concept, when you are hypnotically regressed into your past life or lifetime just prior to the one you are now living, you are actually experiencing the lifetime of your creator. When maneuvered back to the lifetime before that one, you'd be experiencing the life of your creator's creator, . . . etc. In accepting this premise, I believe that hypnotic regressions will take you back through your direct creator lineage; but I also believe that you have the potential through regression to explore or relive the lives of any of the offshoots or branches of that lineage. This, of course, would quickly grow to thousands and probably millions of past life potentials you could reexperience in a hypnotic trance. (See diagram A.)

I'm sure you can see how this belief does not negate a reincarnational belief system and how well it fits in with all the evidence of the parallel concepts. It actually helps to explain many fallacies I have found over the years of conducting past life regressions . . . fallacies in the basic and generally accepted ideas of reincarnation—as an example, the overlapping lifetimes I discussed earlier in the book—the good hypnotic subject who would find himself living two lives within the exact same historic time period . . . and research could verify both existences.

As another example: A good friend of mine is a regressive hypnotist, and after finding a subject reliving a life during the time of Christ, he decided it would be a beautiful project to write the life of Christ through the observations of those who were actually there if enough good subjects could be found. He soon discovered several people who were able to relate vivid details about Jesus. None were key figures in the Passion Play, but they lived during this period and provided numerous details and opinions about the Master. At the time, I felt that the odds were beyond probability and that my friend was not being objective enough in his research work. Yet now, from the perspective I've discussed, it could be quite possible for someone to tap in on a lifetime of any of those on the branches of their spiritual genetic lineage. The probability of a "Jesus-link" might now be within acceptable odds. If the creator concept has validity, it is my theory that in sequential past life regression, you would regress through your "natural" lineage first to

93

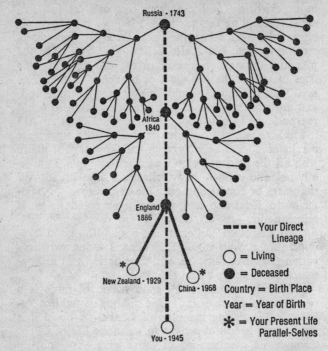

The diagram shows a branching tree structure with the following labels:

Russia - 1743

Africa 1840

England 1886

New Zealand - 1929 *   * China - 1968

You - 1945

- - - - Your Direct Lineage
○ = Living
● = Deceased
Country = Birth Place
Year = Year of Birth
* = Your Present Life Parallel-Selves

(Diagram A) The Creator Concept: Assuming that each individual, upon his death, created only three people as explorations, you can see how rapidly the "V" would widen as it regressed backwards in historic time. It is my theory that in sequential past life regression, you would regress through your natural lineage of spiritual genetics; first to your creator (England, 1886), then to your creator's creator (Russia, 1743), etc. But you have the capability, if directed to do so, to regress to any of the lifetimes within the "V." A strong present-day interest, affinity or ability in common with any of the people in your "V" might cause you under hypnosis, without direction, to return to their lifetime.

NOTE: If you invert the V, you have the "tree of life." If you carry it far enough—going backward in time—you can see how all mankind is related. The concept of the part and the whole becomes much less abstract.

your creator, then to your creator's creator, and so on; but you have the capability, if directed to do so, to regress to any of the lifetimes on the branches. A strong present-day interest, affinity or ability in common with any of those on your branches might cause you, under hypnosis, without direction, to return to their lifetime.

When I've related these ideas in public, many people have gotten upset. "I don't want to think of it that way," is an often-heard remark.

My usual response is, "Then don't!" But what does it really matter? The reason for exposing varying concepts is to open peoples' minds to alternate possibilities and potentials. The moment you close your mind to anything, you stop learning and growing in that area; and if there was ever a subject which requires an open mind, it is metaphysics.

The aversion to this possibility probably lies in the idea of the past lives, not being "my own." Yet, if you are totally affected by them, they really are yours. Another aspect of this rebuttal might be the concept that another individual created you instead of God. In a session with David Paladin in which Wassily Kandinsky was speaking through David, I asked Kandy about the individuals he had created as continuing explorations. He explained that he was now a woman in China, a soldier in Vietnam and many, many others. "I am also still painting in Russia in the 1930's as Wassily Kandinsky. I really enjoyed that period of my life, so I am continuing to explore that potential."

Since Kandy was an artist while living in our reality, I asked him if he was capable of feeding art abilities or art yearnings to the woman he created in China. "All right," he responded, "I'll give you a very simplistic answer—No! She must discover her own creativity; and then once it becomes a co-creative effort, I can assist. Co-creative may be a bad term. She has discovered her own ability to create, then she asks for information, intuitively. She is seeking a broadening of her creative abilities; and at that point, it is agreed that I am not manipulating by saying, 'Here's some concepts I'm going to allow to flow through your head.' But she must choose them. She may be a terrible painter as relates to the Kandinsky identity. She may be a very fine painter as she relates to her own specific identity; but I can't make her paint like Kandinsky or say, 'Be a painter instead of a sculptor, or be a sculptor instead of a musician.' Once she has decided to explore creativity, energy as a whole can feed and support that. The concepts are all there for her to flow through."

THE OVERSOUL CONCEPT

The oversoul concept would claim that you are one of many explorations created by your oversoul. The theory can be viewed from the "no-time, all lifetimes (past, present and future) transpiring at once" perspective. Or from a sequential time perspective of simultaneous multiple incarnations . . . or a combination of the concepts.

According to this belief, you are a part of a complete soul. While in the nonphysical realms, the oversoul decided to explore several physical incarnations. The soul energy was then divided up into several "lives" and the explorations began. You might think of the soul energy as mental abilities. We only use five percent of our brain. Maybe the remaining ninety-five percent contains the totality of the oversoul and all of your parallel-selves? The transfer sessions seem to show that we do have all of the knowledge of our parallels within our mind.

Let's assume that the oversoul exists on a God level and the physical lifetimes are explored as a form of procreation and expansion of the oversoul energy. That would make you like a cell in the body of your God level totality. The part and whole at the same time. Any cell in your present physical body contains your complete "pattern." If our cloning abilities were developed with humans, as is the case with some reptiles, you could be "duplicated" from that cell. So in reality, although you would only be part of your totality from one perspective, from another you are your totality. If the oversoul on the God level is God, or is part of God, then you are God . . . *the part and the whole at the same time.*

This concept, when projected to this degree, does make you God . . . me God. Every living and discarnate individual would be God. Together we could be considered an energy gestalt called God. From my perspective God doesn't exist on a throne in heaven, he is you, and right now he is reading a book.

I question the concepts that are so prevalent in metaphysical teachings of evolving back to God. If we are already him, how do we evolve back to him? Maybe God just wanted to expand his energy by learning new things? Learning is certainly expansion. Maybe physical lives are simply something creative to do? Maybe the goal is simply the exploration of countless billions of creative potentials.

THE TOTAL ILLUSION CONCEPT

This theory would say that life is an illusionary game, created as an evolutive process for the soul, or maybe simply for the fun of it. You are God. You created the entire environment (world) to make the game seem real and to give you limitless possibilities of exploration. Maybe everybody else actually exists, but maybe they are only illusions?

In a hypnotic trance the hypnotised subject can often "totally relive" a past situation. His voice becomes that of a five-year-old and he relives a traumatic situation just as realistically as he did the first time at the age of five. In the trance he interacts with others who are just as real to him as the others he perceives while in a conscious, waking state. From this perspective, your life could be a self-created hypnotic-like illusion.

If that is the case, why did you make it so com-

97

plicated and why give yourself troubles and hangups? How else would you learn anything? How else would it be creative and interesting enough to continue with? There is certainly no challenge in utopia. Most who have found themselves living in a Utopian environment soon report it to be so boring that they often self-destruct, just for something interesting to do.

ENERGY IMMORTALITY CONCEPT

This concept can stand on its own, or can obviously be combined with any of those already discussed. It is based upon contemporary science and some of the experiments going on in the physics laboratories of this country. Scientists are isolating one proton, the elementary particle that is a fundamental constituent of the atom, within a sealed cloud chamber. It cannot get out and nothing else can get in. Naturally it is invisible to the naked eye, but it can be photographed on ultra-high sensitivity film. The researchers have found that the particle has measurable volume and weight. It will go zap, zap, zap in a particular pattern and at a measurable speed. Then it seems to die, dropping to the bottom of the cloud chamber.

What follows is a rebirth, as the film records the same proton rise from the bottom of the cloud chamber. Only now it is going zing, zing, zing. The volume, weight, speed and pattern have changed. It then completes its cycle and repeats the process again and again . . . only differently each time.

This experiment proves that energy cannot die. We are energy. We, like the proton, may be simply exploring potentials. Maybe we are trapped within some form of cloud chamber? That cloud chamber is certainly not the ultimate reality, but is the reality we'll be forced to explore until we figure out how to get out of it. Now, think of the cloud chamber as a reincarnational wheel, which is very real because we decided to give that concept energy and are in the process of exploring it. But an earthly series of reincarnations is certainly not the ultimate reality . . . only one of countless realities.

How would we escape from one reality so we could experience another? Obviously it cannot be done with the body, for the body wears out and dies. Our mind obviously continues through all experiences, for it does contain all of our previous memories. Thus we do not have a mind, we are mind. The continuing and ever-lasting energy that is each of us *is mind*.

Freedom and the creations of new realities would have to be achieved by the mind, and that is the real subject of this book. Other chapters will cover this in considerable detail.

THE ADVANCED SOULS RETURN CONCEPT

This theory hypothesizes that you are an old soul and have reincarnated at this time for a very special opportunity to accelerate your individual evolution. The frequencies of the earth (in our present relation-ship to time/space) have been intensifying for many years, and as this rapid acceleration continues, so will the rate of change and opportunity. Rapid change will cause chaos, and the inability of the masses to adjust will result in an excessive number of world problems. As an old soul you have hopefully learned (intuitively) how to handle these problems and through altruistic endeavors you will evolve.

Many people in metaphysics believe that new souls stopped being born in 1930. Without previous earth lifetimes of experience they would be incapable of adjusting to the intense vibrations of our time. It may be that as the world population gets larger, it is ac-tually getting smaller from a "soul census" supposi-tion; for as the frequency advances, more highly evolved souls, capable of inhabiting ever greater numbers of bodies at the same time, are entering into physical existence. If we all have two parallel-selves, then there are only a third as many souls actually living on the earth at this time.

As a part of this theory, the old souls are here to be part of the forthcoming change. Many psychics are predicting great holocausts and earth changes by the year 2000. The fundamentalist Christians call it Armageddon, and according to them, there will be plagues, pestilence, fire and brimstone.

Others are predicting a transcendance, or some form of frequency switch, which will transpire around the year 2000; and individuals who have freed themselves by rising above fear and accelerating their level of awareness will move forward into a new age of peace and altruism. It will be graduation time.

Those who haven't intuitively learned from their many lifetimes may have to go back and start over in the dark ages and work their way up again.

It can be fun to combine concepts. The Bible says 144,000 will be saved to begin the new age of peace. Assuming this prophecy has validity and can be interpreted from a higher level, it could refer to 144,000 oversouls. Thus from the perspective of parallel-selves that could mean millions of individual people.

THE SCHOOLHOUSE CONCEPT

This is a symbolic theory, provided simply to help you understand how conceivably all of the aforementioned concepts could interrelate and be valid at the same time. It becomes a matter of the "level of interpretation." Let's assume that once upon a time there were no inhabitants on the earth, but there was a great energy gestalt somewhere in the nonphysical realms. That energy may have been the lowly proton with a million universes locked within it, but that is really beside the point. We'll call the gestalt God, but any name would do as well. Now God decided that he wanted to explore, to expand his energy, so he took a great portion of this energy and sent it out in the form of one billion sparks we'll call souls—each a part of the whole, but each individual. Now the souls decided that they needed a reality to explore within, so they chose the earth. The earth would become a school-house, and rules would have to be established. One group of souls voted for sequential time as one of the rules. Another group wanted to evolve within a concept of no time. They all decided that they did not want to be limited to exploring just one physical existence after another.

When all the ideas were in and the final votes taken, the following decisions were made:

1. The schoolhouse would include many class-rooms. These would be every historic period from the first day of school to the last—from the earth's beginnings to the final days, and all would be taught at the same time.

2. To create an illusion of sequential time, there would have to be thousands of frequencies. The rate the electrons or atoms would spin in each frequency would provide the illusion of matter. In other words, any and all square miles of the earth's surface could be used for thousands of different realities. Within the "sequential time" section of the school, a frequency of 100 would be 500 B.C. and the square mile would be desert. At a frequency of 150, the square mile would be 100 A.D. and the square mile would be forest. At a frequency of 450, the square mile would be 1976, and a city would exist there.

3. There would be other realities that could also be explored in the schoolhouse at the same time. Here again, the frequency would dictate the reality, and some souls would evolve with the concept of no time. Others might exist within a totally different horizontal or vertical perception.

4. When the schoolhouse was ready, each soul could begin his explorations, and each would be allowed one thousand physical life choices. Each original soul could not be called an "oversoul," for he would breathe life into each of his thousand choices. He would use his energy to create

more energy by creating people, as we know them, to exist in historic periods. To make the explorations seem real, each individual would enter the physical life with self-inflicted amnesia as to their origin and true reality—although this knowledge would be carried in their cellular structures. Time would relate only as perceived by each of the life creations; and because of the vibrational rate into which they were born, they would be aware only of their own historic frequency or illusion of reality. Actually all other historic periods would be transpiring right in the same physical space; but because of the altered frequency or rate of electron spin, all other time periods would be invisible to sight or touch.

Now please don't take this explanation literally. It is provided as a symbolic concept to illustrate the possibility of the validity of the ideas expressed in the book until now. There are many complicated scientific arguments which could be made to support the basic theory, but I don't feel qualified to express them here. As a simple fact—we only have the ability to see and hear things within very limited audio/video ranges. Try to watch the wings of a hummingbird in flight. At the rate they move they become invisible to your eyes. The book you are now holding in your hand is only a mass of swirling molecules. If the earth's frequency were to switch or if there were no magnetic polarity, the molecules of the book and all other matter would separate and the illusion of reality would no longer exist.

Within this God-gestalt/Souls/Schoolhouse analogy, you can fit all of the concepts in this book—the fact that there is no time, all exists in a constant "now." It expands reincarnation and explains parallel-lives and the creator or oversoul concepts. Both of these can be valid at the same time if you think of the oversoul as the creator of the initial physical life, followed by each exploration creating their own explorations . . .

102

each segment of energy creating more energy, life creating life, just as the cells in your body divide and create more cells.

Reincarnation is the philosophy of life for two-thirds of the world, and continued acceptance by Western societies will soon result in a much higher percentage of believers. The fact that metaphysics (reincarnation and karma) is a workable system of total justice is attractive to people seeking balance in a world of inequality. Theoretically the more advanced souls, now crossing over, are seeking out the religion/science/philosophy that is most conducive to soul evolution.

As the movement grows, so will the organizations to support it. There are already thousands in this country, and although most agree on the basic overview, none agree on the specifics.

Remember that mind is all powerful. Thus what you think and what you believe are extremely important. I always advise that everyone keep a totally open mind and be fully aware that *truth only exists as it relates to you.* If you care to accept any of the existing propaganda and dogma, then it will become your reality, but it will be a self-imposed reality. Real because you gave it validity with the power of your own mind.

CHAPTER 9

KARMA WITHOUT
THE "HOCUS POCUS"

If you were to ask most people if they would like to be released from their negative karma, the answer, without exception, would be a resounding, "Yes!" In asking the same people, "Are you willing to work at it?" most would say, "Yeah . . . well, sure."

We've received hundreds of phone calls during the last year from people who wanted to fly out to Arizona immediately and be hypnotically regressed. "If you can just regress me, I'll know the cause of my problems with my wife and then we'll be able to put our marriage back together."

I proceed to explain that even if we were to find all the causes of his present marital problems through regressive hypnosis into past lives, it would only be the first step to altering the present and future. Sometimes it does help to gain an understanding of the past. Sometimes regressive hypnosis can immediately release subconscious anxieties for one person, but two people are involved in a relationship crisis. Even with the past life knowledge, what you do about the future will still be up to you. Hopefully, it would help you to alter your attitude about the relationship—through additional understanding. But you could certainly proceed to reprogram your reality or rise above your karma without this data.

Before proceeding further, it is important for you to understand how the subconscious mind works, for it is the subconscious we work with in past life recall and positive programming. I want you to think of yourself as a *mind,* for this in reality is what you are. You do not have a mind, *you are mind.* You are the sum total of all of your other lives, which is *all of your past or parallel programming.* You do not consciously remember your other lives because to remember so much would be too overpowering for your present state of awareness to cope with. You were reborn in a state of amnesia, hopefully carrying with you the intuitive knowledge of what is right and wrong for you in this life, so you don't make the same mistakes you've made before.

Your subconscious mind has been active from the moment you were born, and from a reincarnational perspective from the beginning of your physical explorations. *It is your subconscious mind that has made you what you are today.* Your talents and abilities, your problems and afflictions are the result of the intuitive guidance of the subconscious. It has been directing you and it will continue to direct you, often in opposition to your conscious desires. *Why?* The subconscious has little or no reasoning power. . . . It simply operates like a computer, functioning as the result of programming. I call this "karma." Very simply explained, *karma is nothing more than the programming you have created in other lives and your life up until now, and fed into your mind—your own programming of your own computer.*

Now as a medical fact, and this is important: *The subconscious creates only according to programming. It will help to bring into actuality the reality it is programmed for.* Call the programming "karma" . . . and there is nothing occult or mystical about it. Karma is simply a medical fact. If the subconscious received no new programming, it would continue to operate on all of the prior programming of this life and your other lives. This, of course, cannot happen, for you are constantly feeding new data or programming into your computer . . . your subconscious mind. *Every thought* programs the computer. You may be thinking every thought and *action,* but you have to think something before you do it, so we are really speaking of your *thoughts.* If you never conceived a negative thought, you couldn't perform a negative deed.

Every negative or fear thought programs you the other way. So if you are thinking negatively more than positively, you are programming your computer in the wrong way. *You create your own reality (karma) with your thoughts.*

Your thoughts from other lives and your present life up until now have created your "today." If you don't like your today and desire to change it, it is simply time to change your programming . . . your input to the subconscious computer. To look at it another way, it is time to change your karma. I always tell people, "Wisdom erases karma." Ruth Montgomery says, "The law of grace overrides the law of karma." They both mean the same thing. What is wisdom or the law of grace? Simply an expanded awareness or consciousness and the sincere desire to let go of the past and rise above it. The fact that you are sitting there with this book in your hands says that you desire to expand your awareness. There is no instant/magic way to achieve this, but there are ancient and totally effective methodologies for those willing to put forth a consistent effort. *What mind has created, mind can change!* You must have self-discipline and consciously direct and reprogram your subconscious mind to overcome the negative programming of the past.

Many people start off very enthusiastically, determined to follow through and accomplish their desired goals. But they soon run out of steam and begin to slack off in their efforts and then wonder why nothing has happened. *It is my belief that these people are not ready to let go of their negative karma.* For some reason they subconsciously desire to carry the effects forward, and thus they rationalize and procrastinate instead of taking the time to develop the wisdom it takes to rise above their self-inflicted unhappiness and failures . . . purposely hanging on to their problems or failing to accomplish their goals.

If your negative and fear thoughts are resulting in the wrong kind of programming, the first step is quite obvious. You must begin to eliminate all such thoughts from your mind. Easily said and hard to do? Of course it is; but if you want a positive, happy and successful tomorrow, you must start today to make this most important of all changes. In reality, this is the *ultimate wisdom*—the answer of all answers and the Truth of the Universe. It is so simple that most people can't accept it.

Until you begin to monitor your thoughts for negativity, you will have no idea how negative you actually are. Try it for a day. Examine every thought and every verbal utterance. How are you programming your computer?

The woman with a bad marital relationship sits over coffee with her friends: "Oh, I can't stand the way John acts towards me; he has no consideration whatsoever. He expects me to do all the work around here and doesn't appreciate it when I do." This is negative programming, which slowly but surely will result in a more negative relationship. The subconscious can't reason; it only reacts to input. The relationship input is negative, so the subconscious will do its best to assure a negative end result. The subconscious is a very effective machine, which functions to create the reality it comprehends. How does this relate to karma? The husband and wife have probably been together for many lifetimes and they are still trying to achieve a perfected love. When they finally learn that positive programming will create this reality, they will achieve their "soul goal."

Your thoughts, imaginings and fantasies have programmed your karma up until now. If you don't like the results, you must fully realize that you and you alone are responsible for them. The subconscious cannot tell the difference between fact and fantasy . . . between real experiences and imagined experiences.

So if you are allowing fear thoughts to run rampant through your mind, you are certainly moving towards a fearful reality. If you say to yourself, "This marriage is never going to work, I don't see how we'll ever make it," then your subconscious is absorbing that input into the "relationship category" of the computer and it is being received—"Marriage can't work—won't make it." When this computer category is filled to capacity, it will be quite effective in causing the programmed marital failure. The more programming you give it and the faster you provide it, the quicker it will create the reality. Happily for us, positive programming is equally effective.

I often like to quote some of the great men in history who have made statements regarding this power of the mind far more eloquently than I:

Disraeli: "Man is not the creature of circumstances. Circumstances are the creatures of men."

Plato: "We become what we contemplate."

William Blake: "The imagination, the real and eternal world of which this universe is but a faint shadow . . ."

Cudworth: "Mind is senior to the world and the architect thereof."

THE SUBCONSCIOUS MIND IS PROGRAMMED IN TWO WAYS

1. *Karmic programming:* This is the matter of simply living your life as if you had no cosmic control—slowly learning by your mistakes or through your failures. If you had to touch a hot stove 10 times before you learned that it was undesirable to do so, you simply needed 10 painful experiences to reprogram yourself. You may need 10 bad marital relationships, over numerous lifetimes, before you learn to rise above such negative experiences by rejecting negative input.

2. *Conscious programming:* This is a matter of de-

ciding what you want and programming the subconscious mind to help you achieve it.

You have the ability to let go of the past and rise above your negative karma *now!* Change does take time, but now is the time to start. Ask yourself, "Do I *really* want to let go of my negative karma?" "Am I willing to *really* work towards this goal or is it easier to just go on living my life the way it unfolds?"

If you are sincerely willing to work hard towards creating a new reality, you can do it. If you answered the above questions affirmatively and you do not follow through, don't ever complain again about the burdens life has laid on you. You laid them on yourself and you've made the decision that it is easier to accept your lot than expend the energy to create change.

You are mind, which is energy; and through expanded awareness, you can attract and create whatever you want. Things are not given to you, even from a karmic perspective. You are given the power to achieve for yourself the conditions and situations you desire. Who gave you this power? You gave it to yourself through the positive subconscious computer programming in your past. You might say happy and successful people have "good karma." I think of it a little differently. They have carried the intuitive understanding of the power of positive programming from their other lives into their present life. They learned somewhere along the line of reincarnational lineage that "I can't" thinking doesn't work, and "I can and I am" thinking does work.

In the last chapter of this book I will talk about techniques, methodologies and directions for accelerating and intensifying positive reprogramming of the subconscious mind. But remember, the first step is to begin, from this moment on, to eliminate negative-fear thoughts and replace them with positive-love thoughts. As soon as you recognize the negative thought—stop it and cancel it out with a love thought. This way it should never become subconscious computer input. If the thought is about a particular individual, say to yourself, "I love you—I send you love." Even if you hate them—do it! Soon it will be natural, and the positive input will override the old relationship with all of its karmic implications.

CHAPTER 10

THE KINGDON
BROWN SESSION

Kingdon Brown had lectured at several of our past life
seminars during the year, but we'd seldom had time to
discuss our own work and research areas. As one of the
country's finest trance psychics, and a respected metaphysical author of several books, he was usually the
highlight of the seminars. Now, over lunch, we explained the chessboard analogy, our parallel-selves
work and the idea of the frequency switch. "I'm looking for verification, or ways to disprove, some of these
concepts," I explained.

"I don't know what to tell you," Kingdon responded.
"Probably the best way to approach it would be for
me to go into a trance after lunch and see what we
can find out."

He works very much as Edgar Cayce did, self-
imposing a light trance and opening a channel for input, or direct communication, from the other side.
Kingdon was now lying on the couch in his living room,
while Trenna and I sat close by. The decision was
made for him to begin receiving, then later we could
ask him questions.

"You are beginning to understand human advancement from the multiple dimensional point of view. In regard to the chessboard analogy, this is an interchange of energy through the levels of the chessboard, but as the souls transfer the experiences, or the life energies, from one to the other, the essential energies change. What you haven't discovered yet, but are in the process of discovering, is that there is a single reason why civilizations disintegrate and die. You are concerned about the disintegration and wonder if it is a necessary part of human advancement. You wonder if it is not possible for humanity to evolve to a point beyond this physical disintegration. There seems to be a space aspect in this. There are certain individuals in each period of history, in each society, who contain a more conscious recollection of this total life process, or total cosmic operation. They are the key ones around whom the others are grouped, and they are the ones who bring into conscious awareness, as you are doing, these relationships.

"There is also, I feel, . . . although I'm not getting this directly, I'm distilling this so it can be evaluated in a different way. We're also coming into, not only the reality, the constant reality of these other lifetimes, but there is a perspective from another point in the universe operating here. These lifetimes may be . . . oh . . . now I'm getting this very intensely. These lifetimes may be physically manifesting. I don't know how this could be, for it sounds strange to my own mind, but nevertheless I will relate it to you.

"Not only do they live in memory, or in an etheric way, but they may exist in a physical way. There is also the impression that this planet was indeed seeded somehow. That the souls here in physical bodies were brought here, and that we are under some incubation, or gestation, period that has been going on. The reason this is becoming evident is that there is a life-giving continuity here that does not exist elsewhere in the universe in quite this way. The intelligences are still monitoring our progress. I see . . . I'm now getting this directly. It's like a veil or blinders . . . like the Bible says, through a glass darkly. This veil is being removed very carefully to see if we can make this leap, or advancement, without falling backwards into disintegration once again as has happened so many times in history. This is what transcendence means. We become something else. There is an experiment going on with this planet and the intelligences that are observing it are not taking part directly, for it happens automatically at a certain point. They are observing to see if this time we can accept evolutionary knowledge and true change. There is something here about the relationship of all your past, present and future physical explorations transpiring in a constant now, and that you will all have to make this change at once. . . . Everybody has to make it. An instantaneous thing . . . without falling back again into a dark age, or a point where all is hidden once again.

"Now, let's get back to the chess board once again. The question is, are the past, present, or future lifetimes causative on each other? Is it a mutual causality . . . is Trenna influencing the others, or are they influencing her, or is it both? The others are deposited within her. There is a static quality to them. She is a compilation of the others but she modifies. In other words history is constantly being rewritten, or modified, because we do have the ability to influence the past and thus the past changes. The way you look at a memory in a different way as you grow older . . . something that happened as a child seems to be different, when viewed from the age of fifteen than from the age of twenty-five, etc. The physical event remains static, but it is perceived in a different light as you grow. So we are all modifying the other levels of the chess board. All human history is moving. On some levels there are aspects of ourselves that are not evolv-

113

ing as well, so we have to pull them along by intuitively, or by subconsciously, influencing. It is not higher, in the sense of being better, or worse than, because we all have to go through it . . . it's not a hierarchy. It's gradual stages of self-revelation which leads to the self-revelation of the others. So the self really isn't the self after all. The self is a compilation and is attempting to evolve, or move, towards something."

(Kingdon now seems very confused and then shocked by what is coming in. Three or four minutes pass.) "Well, I'll have to say this the way it comes to me, but it seems incredible to me. I can't censor it because that would defeat the purpose of this. We are moving towards a point of 'etherealisation'. . . . Ah, we don't really have a word for it in English. We are attempting to move to a place where we do not exist in physical bodies, yet we exist in an etheric way in which all is totally clear to us . . . as to what has transpired and why we then exist. I'm also receiving with this . . . this is the reason it's so difficult for me to comprehend . . . that at some point when we have reached this degree of evolution, a decision will then be made as to whether or not it will be necessary to continue this planet. It will either be entirely destroyed . . . or something. What I'm seeing visually is that all of these souls that have been interconnected here and interrelated are fragmenting out the way a dandelion seeds out, and they are going out everywhere. I'm being told that this is why this is an incubating place, where all this care has been placed through centuries of bringing human beings past the state of experimentation into the point of self-creating. . . . But they are self-perpetuating in an etheric way, or through a spiritual essence, an astral essence. We create spiritually . . . spiritual propagation . . . ah, that is love. Love is a propagating of the spiritual nature. We will no longer recreate in the way we do now, for we no longer need these bodies, but are in light bodies, and we propagate in a vibration that we call love. We are

114

evolving through a natural process, learning to move into this state without falling backwards.

"You are being shown the model of human evolution, or human advancement in consciousness. It seems the way I'm receiving this, that it is a matter of moving from what we call the physical into the spiritual. I'm being told that is not entirely correct. Wherever I'm getting this from they are agitated that I'm not saying it right. Strike that. They say there is no such demarcation. It is a . . . I'm being told that I'm getting into something sensitive here. I don't know what they mean by that. I don't even know if it is 'they,' or who they are exactly. All right, I'm going to leave this alone. Just a minute, let me bring myself up just a little and then you may ask me questions. . . . o.k."

Dick: Kingdon, I'm interested in any more information you might be able to provide on the transcendence, or maybe frequency switch. From what you said I perceive that we are presently evolving through many interrelated physical explorations which are all transpiring at the same time . . . towards a goal of transcendence.

Kingdon: This etherealisation is the transcendence and is the same as a frequency switch. It can be done while we keep our physical bodies, but we can also do it without these bodies. This may be at the point at which it is attenuated, and that is why it is an experiment. We have to learn how to avoid falling backwards. Through our own evolution we help our otherselves to evolve and thus the total soul will complete the transcendence. There is a telepathic channel, or link, between you and those you consider your past lives, or parallel-selves. You are all on a similar plane of understanding, but it is not always understanding in a conscious way.

There is a connecting principle. It is like men in an army . . . a line going across a field. They're all going across the same field, but they are separate soldiers, but they are related because their purpose and objec-

115

tive is the same. It would be accurate to say that they come from the same creative emitase, just as a shooting star starts off as one stream of light and then it breaks up into individual pieces as it comes into the atmosphere and explodes. They come from the same soul creation, but they fragment into individual parts. All are in the same stages, however not physically. It requires another dimension to evaluate it.

Dick: So we are all affecting all of our counterparts, and hopefully we are evolving towards a higher level of awareness which will result in transcendence?

Kingdon: Yes . . . yes . . . they are affecting each other and are in constant superconscious communication with each other at all times. They feel the same things, but the forms and circumstances in which they feel are different, but the effects, or results of their experiences, from an overview, are the same. The same experiences, but through different forms. Those more evolved are trying to influence the rest in an attempt to get to this point. There is definitely a progression involved here, which is a new idea for me. You are on the right track with this.

Dick: How do we relate to those in our own future? Would this be an evolutive, reincarnational cycle, or simply another fragment of our own soul exploring in a constant now?

Kingdon: The future exists now. Interplanetary visitors move in time and space. Time and Space are not two separate realities, or two separate dimensions, they are actually part of the same dimension. What I am now getting is also very strange to me. It is not really reincarnation, for it is also procreation. We are not only receiving the influence of the past, but we're also receiving the influence of what is ahead in the future. We need a new word for reincarnation to describe this. Our own past and future are being felt and the result is a blending. There's a forward, evolutive movement here. Perhaps this is what karma is, ah . . . karma is not working out something from the past the way we used to think of it. It is a molding of the past, present and future into the progression . . . the evolution that is forthcoming. I also seem to be receiving something to the effect that perhaps the word soul is not correct either. It might be better to use the term "creative impulse." A creative impulse that upon entering into the physical, fragments into many pieces. Our concept of time and space is erroneous to the extent that it doesn't seed unity . . . Since they are one and the same, simultaneous multiple life explorations can transpire, each within its separate dimension, and through our multiple explorations progression results. Once this is understood, revelation can follow. The veil can be lifted. That is what has been happening with you and Trenna.

(End of this portion of the session.)

Upon pulling himself up out of his transcended level of consciousness, Kingdon sat up on the couch and shook his head. "Boy oh boy! I don't know about some of that. I don't know if I helped you or not?"

"When I get a chance to pull some copies of the other chapters in the book, you'll see how you've substantiated our other material from an alternate perspective and have also injected some new concepts," I replied.

In the car on the way home we discussed it all further. "What do you think?" Trenna asked.

"It makes sense. Athenna is a little more evolved than you, but as you developed your own awareness, she found a channel for direct, in addition to subconscious, influence. Of course you're also helping her and together working to pull all of your separate selves towards a transcendence. Another thing, think of how often we've tapped in on these 'light beings' or 'light people'? We have to have at least twelve to fifteen regressions of other people where we've accidentally touched on this, just as have several other regressive hypnotists we've talked to." (An incident in a past life seminar, involving Trenna and a woman from San Francisco, nearly caused a ballroom full of people to panic and took Trenna two days to throw off the effects. This will be the subject of a later chapter.)

"I know," she said, staring blankly out the window. "I think without realizing it, Kingdon has just unlocked and started to open a bigger door."

CHAPTER 11

PSYCHIC ABILITIES
AND GUIDANCE

Everyone is psychic; they simply do not recognize their own ability. With proper direction, followed by dedication to development, any individual will soon see the manifest results of their sixth sense. Some people develop faster than others, just as they would in learning to play tennis. But as in tennis, if you learn the basics and are willing to devote some time and effort to developing your interest, you will soon be able to play a fair game.

Such personal development is not without its share of problems. Whenever anyone tells me that they want to develop their psychic abilities, I ask them quite bluntly, "Why?"

"Oh, because it would be so neat to be psychic," is a very standard reply. My usual comeback is, "Well, I can show you how, but believe me it can be a problem that can complicate your life. If you have enough problems now, don't pursue this form of expanded awareness." Such advice usually goes unheeded.

I have found that when people develop their understanding of metaphysical concepts and become involved in new age activities, psychic abilities soon follow quite naturally. Trenna has always been psychic, but through her constant intensive work in seminars, with individuals, and the contacts with Athenna, she literally "blew open," as I call it. She developed an extremely high degree of accuracy as a telepath, and in a hypnotic trance she was close to total accuracy on psychic information that could be validated. The new abilities necessitated her learning new techniques to shield herself when in groups and developing defensive techniques which would help her to coexist in a normally nonpsychic world. She made the mistake of psychically opening on the sidewalks of New York City, "to feel the totality of the environment." The experience sent her reeling up against a building with her hands on her ears.

"You can do that in Arizona, but I don't think I'd explore that particular technique here," I said. She agreed.

A woman from Ohio came to a Scottsdale seminar and psychically opened overnight. Before the week was over, she was accurately picking up the thoughts of others and could tell people things she consciously had no way of knowing. She was experiencing many paranormal situations. I tried to talk to her about "shielding" and protective measures which could help to shut down the mental input when it was undesirable. "What are you being so fearful about, Dick? I can handle this beautifully," was her reaction.

Two days later I received a phone call asking for the advice I'd tried to offer previously. On the airplane going home, she was sitting next to a man in the process of divorce and proceeded to pick up his feelings and depressions. At home she was immediately involved in some very undesirable family situations, resulting in far more negative input than she normally would have experienced without the empathic abilities.

One evening we were sitting around the swimming pool of a Scottsdale resort with a group of people. One moment Trenna was happy and involved in the conversation, the next she jumped up. "Something has happened to Grizzly," she said, almost in a panic. "I'm going back to the room to call Sally (a neighbor)." Sally told her that Griz, one of our dogs, and Trenna's favorite, had been violently killed at exactly that time.

120

"I had a talk with him about a week ago," she said, crying. "I remember asking him why he had to leave? He was only a year old. I knew it was going to happen."

I do not want to leave the reader with the impression that psychic ability is a negative. It can have complications, as I have pointed out, but we have received innumerable positive and helpful pieces of information and guidance over the years through psychic channels and methodologies.

A few situations involving Athenna and healing are perfect examples. Trenna has always been very prone to throat infections, often resulting in strep. Once it starts, it always runs the full course, which is usually a week. On one occasion, the infection had set in. She had accepted the inevitable, but Athenna came through to Trenna in the form of an inner voice, without the induction of a trance. "Put a blue scarf around your neck. The color will help to heal. Use your self-hypnosis techniques to visualize yourself as healed and have Dick mentally send blue light to your throat everytime he looks at you. We'll be helping from over here." The next morning the infection was completely gone.

A similar situation developed just two days before we were to fly to Dallas, Texas, for a seminar. I'd been in a Phoenix recording studio all day cutting new masters for a line of hypnosis tapes that are marketed by a Phoenix publishing company. I arrived home late at night, very tired. Trenna was in bed and explained that the throat infection had really hit her. She didn't have the energy to sit up. "I've been using the blue cloth and the other techniques all afternoon, but it's obviously getting worse," she explained.

"Let me go into hypnosis for a few minutes," I said. "I'll try to get myself relaxed and pull in my energy; then maybe I can work on it too." A few years before I'd practiced at developing healing power in my hands, to help work with a critically burned young man. I felt I might be able to do the same thing again.

Once in hypnosis I used my own techniques to

begin to relax and was just about to awaken when I received a direct communication not to. It was coming through my own Guide contacts, but I felt the information was being directed from Athenna. "Remain in the trance and begin to imagine the healing energy developing in your hands. They will get hotter and hotter as this happens." I did as directed and soon my hands felt as if I were holding hot coals. The inner voice continued. "Now speak up and tell Trenna (who was lying beside me on the bed) to remove the scarf from her neck and to remain quiet. Now, without opening your eyes, or breaking the trance, I want you to sit up and place both of your hands on her neck." I did as directed. "Now imagine the healing power flowing out of your body; feel the pulsation as this transpires. Also imagine a blue light flowing from your mind down through your arms and into your hands. This blue light is flowing into your wife's throat."

After a few minutes I rolled back over and lay down, proceeding to count myself up out of the trance. Once more awake, I looked at Trenna. "I could feel heat and a pulsation," she explained. Five minutes later she was up and out of bed. "I feel fantastic . . . come on, lazy bones, what are you doing relaxing when we have so many things to do before tomorrow?" I won't repeat my response to that, but on examining her throat, I saw that the infection was obviously still there. Yet she was feeling none of the effects. By the next morning her throat was perfectly normal.

Subsequent attempts have not always been as successful. Why it works so well one time and to a lesser degree the next I am not sure. Maybe both people have to be tuned in on the same psychic wavelength for maximum results. It does seem, though, that we are always able to at least mitigate, or accelerate, negative physical effects.

I've found in my years of working with groups of people that about eight to ten percent have highly developed empathic abilities. Most of them do not realize it. In public demonstration sessions in which Trenna does psychic monitoring, I often ask those in the audience to attempt it themselves. As an average, ten out of every hundred will easily comply.

Trenna developed her monitoring abilities to help me derive the maximum information from hypnotic sessions with individuals who came to us for help. By going into a light trance along with the subject I was hypnotising, she could advise me about upcoming regression events and alert me when the subject's subconscious was trying to avoid reliving a painful situation. This would usually be something very traumatic that had taken place in a previous lifetime, and the subject's subconscious mind was trying to avoid telling bad things on itself.

Most subjects become observers of their own past by seeing prior life situations unfold before their own inner eyes. Trenna totally relives the past life situation, which can result in a far more dramatic regression, but also is a tremendous emotional drain.

In working with a Hollywood entertainer who had come to Prescott for an all-day regression session, Trenna once experienced more than even she was willing to take on. The woman was in a recliner in a deep trance and was reliving a very negative aspect of one of her own past lives. Trenna was sitting directly behind me in a light trance, monitoring the session. She handed me a note. "She's going to kill herself. I think she'll hang herself!" I noticed that Trenna was holding her throat as if it were hurting, then she grabbed her stomach and almost fell out of the chair. Two minutes later the subject did experience death at her own hands, only she had taken poison to escape the miserable situation in the previous lifetime.

Trenna explained after the session: "I was perceiving the suicidal thoughts, then the pain hit my throat and blocked the impressions I was receiving. I assumed death by hanging. What I was probably receiving was the feeling of the poision as it burned the throat, then a few seconds later the painful sensation when it reached her stomach."

Many new age thinkers feel that we are moving into

a time when psychic abilities will be the "norm," just as our five senses are today. They feel that telepathic communication will be the evolutionary outcome of metaphysical acceptance, and the movement is just beginning to take form in the United States.

For many years Arizona has been the rapidly developing psychic center of the country and now far exceeds Virginia Beach in the number of organizations and activities. This psychic concentration is within a one-hundred-mile circle that includes Phoenix, Scottsdale, Sedona and Prescott. Phoenix, of course, is well known. Sedona is an "arty" and extremely wealthy community of five thousand people nestled in the giant red rocks that have served as the background for hundreds of western movies. There is more psychic activity per capita here than in any city in the country. Prescott is a typical old Arizona cowboy town of 18,000 people situated in a mountain valley and surrounded by national forest.

People from everywhere are being directed psychically to come here. Many involved in Eckankar are being told on "the inner plane" to relocate in Prescott/Sedona (sixty driving miles apart) and they have moved their entire families thousands of miles because they felt it was important. Also psychic practitioners, writers and simply those dedicated to the philosophy are coming in increasing numbers.

In Los Angeles an old Sioux Indian woman—a shaman who had once worked with Black Elk—told me, "I've had a great vision and in it Chief Gall came to me and told me to go to Arizona. It was here that the movement would form and spread. An Indian symbol would guide the way."

Brad Steiger was one of our guest speakers during a portion of the spring–summer 1977 seminar tour. As an author of over fifty books on the psychic and supernatural, he is certainly one of the country's metaphysical leaders. Trenna and I sat with Brad and his fiancee, Francie, in an Atlanta restaurant. Francie is a counselor and psychic channel who has been the subject of articles in most of the new age magazines. "We're moving to Arizona," Brad explained. "Francie has received so much direction from spirit that we can't ignore it any longer. We'll be out there to stay in July."

A new family from Florida recently moved into an A-frame cabin in Groom Creek, above Prescott. They are actively involved in this work and explained that a psychic began telling them to come here a year ago, even accurately describing the home they would buy.

Whenever I ask the newcomers why, the answer is always, "We were told to come." There are many psychic migration theories and none of them negates the others, so all could be valid. Most have to do with "energy." In the Bradshaw Mountain area some say it is the mountain top elevation and the pine trees. Pine trees are supposed to provide more life energy to the atmosphere than any other plant or tree. It is a somewhat generally accepted belief that if you stand on the north side of a pine tree and hug it, you will be "recharged." I don't know if I accept that or not, but it is an interesting idea and I've been known to hug a few myself.

Many feel that something is supposed to happen here or from here. Sedona is supposedly situated over an ancient Lemurian city, and anyone who is at all psychically sensitive will feel the intensity of the vibrations in this area. As a fact: Couples who move here either develop their relationship far beyond the original unity or they rapidly "come-apart" and go separate ways. There is something about the energy source of the area that no one understands. Phoenix has always been known as "the valley of healing," even by the original Indians who settled here. A "special" energy is again given as the reason. There are now approximately two hundred psychic churches or organizations based in the area: and any night of the week, you have your choice of countless activities.

Another concept is that all great religions or spiritual philosophies have been launched from desert areas. Supposedly desert energy is conducive to evolutive

125

thinking. Prescott and Sedona are high desert, and Phoenix is a saguaro desert area.

Lyall Watson, the author of *Supernature,* is a biologist who investigates metaphysical concepts in his latest book, *The Romeo Error*. The following is a direct quote from that book: "Navigation is bedeviled by the fact that the earth's magnetic field is riddled with local deviations and irregularities. These faults have been very carefully plotted and the most persistent of them have become quite notorious. One of these lies off the Bahama Islands (the Bermuda Triangle), another in the English county of Sussex, and a third near Prescott in Arizona."

After much investigation and with considerable help from psychically oriented individuals, Trenna and I found the energy vortex in our own area. Actually, it is much closer to Sedona than to Prescott. The lady who took us to the site provided the following warning, "Whatever you do, don't go down into it. I brought a friend here once and we just sat on the edge for about an hour. When we got home, he had large blisters on the bottom of his feet and he hadn't felt a thing while we were there. I wouldn't let my own feet hang over the edge for anything." She then left us and returned to her home in Sedona.

The area was simply a large depression in the giant red rocks. Cactus and desert growth were thriving in it as well as on the rest of the mountain side. At one side of the depression was a cliff edge, dropping several hundred feet to a valley below. The view from here was magnificent.

I decided to go back to the pickup, parked off the road about a half a mile away to get pen and paper to make notes. Trenna remained on the edge of the vortex. When I returned, she was standing with both hands up, palms out, facing the depression. "Here, I want you to try this," she said. "Put your hands up like this and tell me what you feel."

I did as she asked. "There's a force or pressure. I can feel it in my palms."

126

"All right, now face away from it and do the same thing," she continued. "Now what do you feel?"

"Nothing. Absolutely nothing."

"Looks like it's for real," was our combined opinion. After discussing our inner feelings about the advisability of going down into the vortex, we both agreed it was the correct thing to do. This was the beginning of three beautiful hours which are hard to describe.

At first Trenna went into a light trance and received the following direct writing: "Whispering Voices was the Indian's name for this place. According to legend, Indian lovers believed they could hear a mere whisper in the valley if they stood there. Therefore, it became a place of power to them. They call their spirits here."

Library research provided the following substantiation (from *Sedona Life* magazine, "Religion of the Red Mountains," by Heather Hughes):

> Indian legend tells us that there are four places in the world designated as "power spots" and that these four are broken into two plus two—two positive and two negative or two "light" and two "dark." It is believed that the two "positive" places in the world are Kauaii, an island in Hawaii . . . and Sedona, both red-rock countries. Sedona and Kauaii, the Indians say, are vortexes of energy in which the Great Spirit gives birth to rainbows.
>
> Indians tell us that the towering crimson peaks stimulate sensitivity and that here a man realizes his true dreams and ambitions. They also say that the mountains are like a great magnet and that people are drawn to them because it is the home of the Great Spirit. Amid red-rock country, it is said that man comes face to face with himself and the potentials of his nature.

Our next experiment while in the vortex was for me to hypnotise Trenna and let her roam free in a deep trance to see what impressions might come in. She was soon describing a situation between the Indians and the U. S. Army which transpired in the valley below, as seen by a young Indian named Grey Cloud. The incident was unimportant, so would not be historically recorded; but as Trenna talked, her hands began to move gracefully, and it was soon obvious that she was using Indian sign language to relate the story along with her words. She had become an Indian or was imitating the actions she was observing. Her English became very broken and forced.

Next I went into a self-imposed hypnotic trance and received many dancing visions that would be of little value to relate here. We made love on the rocks in the sunny September afternoon and Trenna received vivid impressions of an entity who would one day be our child.

By the time the sun was going down, we both felt we had received enough of whatever unseen force was emanating from the vortex. There were no adverse physical or mental effects. In fact, as an interesting side note on this day—I was one day into a case of stomach flu that was hitting everyone in our area at the time. Most felt the effects for four days or more. Yet on emerging from the vortex, all signs of the flu were gone and I experienced no more of it.

Maybe it is "energy" that is pulling people together. Past life soul-grouping energy, some cosmic energy as in the Sedona vortex, or the mental energies of like-minded people. It doesn't matter how, only that there is an evident momentum, and it is not happening just in Arizona. In touring nationally, I've found intense centers everywhere. The mail I've received from readers also supports the idea of "psychic hot spots." A few of the primary ones are: Dallas and Houston, Texas; Seattle, Washington; Milwaukee, Wisconsin; Chicago and Rockford, Illinois; and Southern California, although much of the California movement is migrating to Arizona. The large number of people in New York City makes it an area of heavy interest, but not a developing migratory center. Virginia Beach, Virginia, is naturally the east coast center of metaphysical interest, primarily due to the A. R. E. which is located there (the Edgar Cayce Association for Research and Enlightenment).

In *You Were Born Again to Be Together* I talked about personal Arizona regroupings that related back to a massacre at Alamos, Mexico, and before that to the ancient city of Teotihauacan. Since that book was published, I've met many others from Alamos and their stories are fascinating and supportive. Others have written to me with evidence of similar regroupings. In one case it was a Catholic priest in Greenland who used psychic methodologies to substantiate his concepts. Another came from a woman in Bermuda who offered much evidence to support her belief.

If these things are happening by "plan," then I feel it is your plan and only through your own acceptance will changes occur. You will certainly never be forced to develop psychic abilities, or find out about your past lives and associations, or to relocate to a metaphysical geological location. You control and create your reality, in these things as in all others.

CHAPTER **12**

CASE HISTORY:
BOB AND MARY—
PAST LIFE REGRESSION
AND PHYSICAL HEALING

In early June, 1976, I received a phone call from a
Kansas City business man named Bob————. He
explained that he had read my book and wished to
fly out for a private regression session. His wife had
left him, and he was in the process of deciding if he
should divorce her. A series of separations and hard
times over their eight years of marriage had worn him
down; and as much as he loved his wife, he felt on the
verge of letting go. "I feel if I can just learn the reason
for our problems, I can accept the situation easier."

At the time I was taking only a small percentage
of the people calling for private appointments, but
something in the back of my mind told me to say "yes."
We visited for awhile, and I told Bob if he was willing
to come all the way down to the Bradshaw Mountains, I'd schedule a day to work with him, explaining
the fees, the conditioning tape I'd send him, and the
fact that even if we were to find the causes of his
present marital problems through regressive hypnosis
into past lives, it really wouldn't change the present or
future. Almost as an afterthought, I added, "If there is
any possible way to talk your wife into coming along,
I think it might help."

The plan: Bob would fly to Phoenix in two weeks,

arriving on a Friday afternoon. He would rent a car and drive to Prescott, where we'd made motel reservations. Trenna and I planned to have dinner with him Friday evening if we were free . . . then spend all day Saturday doing regression work.

Bob called upon his arrival in Prescott. "I talked Mary into coming with me!" He sounded as excited as a schoolboy. We agreed to meet at the motel and arrived a couple of hours later—meeting Bob and Mary for the first time in a motel room filled with fresh red roses.

"Oh, Bob's always doing things like that," Mary explained. "Sometimes he sends me so many roses I can't find enough vases to put them in." She spoke in a very soft Southern accent.

Over dinner in a local restaurant, we learned more about them and their relationship. Bob is forty-six; Mary, fifty-three, although I'd have guessed her age at around forty to forty-five. Both had been previously married and had children from their early marriages. One of Mary's daughters, a teenager, lived with them.

"I put the old salesmanship to work and talked her into coming along with me," Bob explained, putting his arm around his wife, who snuggled into his shoulder and smiled. "Of course, my salesmanship is what gets me in trouble with her sometimes," he added.

"How's that?"

"Well, she thinks everything is a 'line' . . . even the fact that I love her. I don't think I've ever convinced this beautiful little lady that I *really* love her," he said, smiling at Mary.

"Oh, it's just that Bob is always selling. That's why he's so successful. But I guess he's right . . . I've never really been sure! I should be, I know, but there's always something in my mind that makes me doubt his love."

They went on to explain the circumstances that led up to this most recent of separations. I was waiting for the basis of the problem to surface in our conversation, yet nothing but general incompatibility and too much possessiveness was revealed.

131

Trenna was talking with Mary. "What about feeling possessive, Mary? Can you explain that a little more?"

"I admit that I'm far too possessive and it gives Bob a hard time. The stewardess on the airplane seemed to ignore me as we were boarding, looking right past me at Bob, who was a ways behind. I thought about turning around and saying, 'Do you have the passes, honey?' to Bob. That would have put the flirting stewardess in her place; but anyway, I resisted the temptation."

Bob was obviously agreeing with her interpretation of the event, but wasn't about to comment on it.

"Why did you leave this time, Mary?" I asked directly.

"We just weren't happy and I'm always so afraid of Bob's temper."

"Has the relationship ever been violent?"

"Oh no; he's grabbed me a couple of times when he's really been mad, but he's never hurt me . . . yet . . ." She was looking at Bob.

"Go ahead and tell them," Bob said.

"Well, I'm always afraid Bob's going to kill me. It's always in my mind that when we're not getting along he's going to get mad and kill me! That's much of the reason I left this time."

"And you have no known reasons for these fears, Mary?"

"No, Dick. I was no sooner gone this time . . . went to my daughter's home in Kentucky, which is where I lived before meeting Bob. Anyway, I was no sooner there than he has five dozen red roses being delivered to the door."

We talked more about their relationship and it became quite obvious to me that they both sincerely wanted it to work. After eight years of marriage, Bob was obviously still totally infatuated with his wife. While the ladies were in the rest room, he told me, "Your wife is really beautiful, Dick, with a perfect figure; but I wouldn't trade five of her for my Mary! I wish she could get past this fear and possessiveness though . . . I mean, I really love her. I don't want anyone else. While Trenna was telling us a story during the dinner, she kept looking at me . . . and it made me nervous. I was thinking inside, 'Oh please look at Mary instead, I don't want her to feel funny.' I know there's nothing to a woman looking at me during a conversation like that, but I'm always worried about Mary's reaction."

The rest of the evening was spent talking about psychic work and metaphysical philosophy. We then returned Bob and Mary to their motel and supplied them with a map of how to find us in the mountains the following morning.

Saturday A.M.—It was Bob who desired the regressive experience, but Mary wanted to sit in on the sessions. We all talked for about an hour and Bob supplied me with a lengthy list of questions he hoped could be answered through past life and Higher-Self awareness.

He was a good subject with a medium/deep hypnotic ability. The first session was preliminary past life exploration. Once he was hypnotized, I instructed his subconscious mind to choose a lifetime that would be of value in understanding present relationship ties. He successfully regressed to a very emotional lifetime in the 1200's, in what would now be Switzerland. The regression revealed an important past-life tie with his father—and they share a very close relationship in this life. It was enlightening in other personality areas too, but I felt his subconscious was avoiding the issue. They had traveled half way across the country because of a relationship crisis in their personal life. Bob should have experienced something more important.

He had already been in hypnosis for nearly an hour, so I decided to do a scan regression before awakening him. (Instructions given.)

Q. You are now going to touch in only upon past times in which you have known your present wife, Mary. I now want you to move to a past life in which the two of you have been together.

133

A. I see ancient Egypt . . . I see the pyramids . . . I'm in a crowd.

Q. What else can you tell me about yourself?

A. I'm a learned man . . . I have long flowing robes, very colorful . . . I have all kinds of jewelry . . . wealth and power . . . I don't know who I am . . . I'm there . . .

Q. Is Mary there with you?

A. She is there . . . I see her in a big room . . . a bed . . . it has a high canopy . . . silk . . . she's there.

Q. All right, let's move forward to another lifetime in which the two of you have been together. (Instructions given.)

A. There is a time in early America . . . frontier . . . we farm . . . we farm. We try to make something out of the wilderness . . .

Q. Tell me about the pictures you are perceiving at this time.

A. A cabin . . . and a clearing . . . cleared for farming . . . it looks . . . I'm losing the picture . . .

Q. If there is another lifetime the two of you have been together, I want you to move to that time. (Instructions given.)

A. I see the French court.

(End of first session.)

I still had the feeling Bob was avoiding the issue. "Let's work with some Higher-Self hypnosis after we take a little break. Then we'll come back to the past-life ties."

Although Higher-Self work is not always successful with unconditioned subjects, he responded well to my initial questions. Through this session, which seemed to incorporate information from his own Masters and Guides, Bob was able to answer many questions about his present life and much future life direction was revealed. Tears streamed down his cheeks as he responded to my questions about what he should be doing with his life from this time on. In regard to

Mary, he should be, "patient and more loving and understanding." "A selfless, perfected love." But we received nothing that would provide insight as to the original cause of their problems.

Trenna had fixed an oversized Mexican lunch of sour cream enchiladas, and the four of us discussed the morning sessions. "I'm receiving very strong impressions to ask you to go into hypnosis, Mary," I told her. "Are you willing to do this?"

She had already discussed the possibility with Bob and was agreeable.

MARY
Regression Session

She was instructed to go back to a past life in which she and Bob had been together before and one that would help to explain their present circumstances.

Mary initially saw herself living in Austria as a teen-aged boy. When instructed to move forward to an important event, she became upset, for it was the time of her grandfather's death. She began crying and had to be given very calming suggestions. "He died, he just got old and died!"

When moved forward in time again she became confused, for she now saw herself as a girl. "Oh, I'm a girl now . . . no! . . . No! I'm a girl! I'm a girl! Flowers and perfume . . . I don't understand . . . I don't . . . "

At this point I decided to move the subject into the Higher Self to try to achieve a better understanding of the situation. (Instructions given.)

Q. I now want you to speak up and explain this situation to me.
A. I was masquerading as a boy . . . to please my grandfather . . . my grandfather wanted a grandson.

135

Q. After your grandfather died, did you continue to play a male role?

A. Only for a little while.

Q. What did you learn from this?

A. My grandfather helped me ... helped me to be a girl ... his spirit ... *his* spirit helped me to be a girl.

Q. Is there anything that you can communicate to me about the importance of this particular lifetime or the tie with your present husband Bob?

A. I thought Bob wanted a boy ... oh no ... no ... It's crazy ... Is Bob my grandfather? ... Bob *is* my grandfather!

Q. I want to know what you felt towards your grandfather. Did you love him very much?

A. Oh, yes!

Q. Did you fear your grandfather?

A. Oh no, he was gentle and kind ... but I wanted to be what he wanted me to be.

Q. I now want you to allow more understanding to come in. Your own Guides and Masters are there helping you and I want you to receive more understanding about this situation.

A. Oh no! *Bob's mean!* He's mean! He's going to hurt me. *He's going to hurt me. He's going to kill me!*

(At this point, Mary completely loses control and begins to scream, kick and thrash around, causing the microphone to fly across the room. I instantly restrained her and removed her from the mental environment. Calming suggestions were given and the trance deepened.)

Q. All right now, I want the understanding; and you have the ability, only as an observer, to tell me what this was all about. Now you are blowing out something that has been needed to be blown out for a long time. These emotions have been pent up for entirely too long, and we are now going to get to the bottom of this. You are going to let go of the past through reexperiencing it. Tell me now what happened.

A. I'm not mad at Bob, he didn't mean to kill me . . . he didn't mean too . . . he just got over me . . . and got mad . . .

Q. Where were you when this happened?

A. The apartment in Glen Oaks . . . near St. Louis . . . the couch in the living room . . . I fear he was going to kill me . . . if I'd stayed there he would have . . . oh my goodness . . . that's why I left.

Q. How long ago did this happen?

A. Three years ago. He really wanted to kill me.

Q. But he did not hurt you?

A. No.

Q. This was only your own fear thoughts, right?

A. Well, he had someone else . . . *another woman* . . . another woman . . . he wanted to kill me . . . he wanted to get me out of the picture so he could have her.

Q. (I glanced over at Bob, who was sitting about three feet away. His eyes were as big as saucers and he shrugged his shoulders in disbelief.) Now this is only your own fear, a fear that has manifested and grown and I now want you to let go of this. Completely let go of this and *you are going to move backward in time to the very beginning of this problem* . . . Be it in this lifetime or a past life, you are now going to move backward in time to the very beginning of this problem. It is time to let go of the past and move forward into an environment of love . . . so you are going to go back to the beginning so you will understand this fear. (Instructions given.) I now want you to speak up and tell me what you perceive.

A. He's got a suit on . . . like Caesar . . . a lance with a big wide sword on it . . . he's, he's *cutting off my head* . . . *cutting right through my necklace* . . . (calming suggestions given) . . . *cutting my head off!*

Q. What had you done that caused him to do this?

137

A. I was unfaithful . . . I had a lover . . . I had a
lover . . . he said I did . . . I don't know who it
was, but he said so . . . he said I did . . . *oh, I
know now what it is!* I know what it means . . .
He said I did and I didn't . . . *and I said Bob
did and he didn't!*

I now removed Mary from the situation and gave
her intensive calming and positive suggestions about
the future.

(End of session.)

Obviously Bob, in some ancient time, had acted in
anger because of a suspected infidelity and killed Mary.
The subconscious anxiety had carried forward in the
form of her unwarrented fear of his anger. Her resent-
ment at being accused of having a lover, when in fact
she did not, had resulted in her own similar accusations
in their current relationship.

By the time this lengthy session was completed,
everyone involved was exhausted. It was already
6:00 P.M. and it took another half hour before Mary
felt capable of standing up. They had found the answers they were seeking and it would now be up to
them to rise above what had transpired in the past.

The next day I cut a special self-hypnosis programming tape I wanted them to work with together at
home. It would help them to keep their minds focused
upon the positive aspects of their relationship and incorporate occult protection techniques to shield them
from a considerable amount of outside negative influence they experienced in their environment of
family, friends and associates.

A few weeks later I received a phone call from
Bob and Mary. "I've never felt so free in my life,"
she explained. "All the old fear is gone and I know
inside it won't come back. We're together and doing
fine. I feel we'll make it."

Bob went on to ask me about real estate in Arizona.
"We felt so peaceful while we were there that we

want to get a place to come to and maybe eventually plan to move there. I feel it's time to think about doing more important things than running a successful business."

Late that summer they returned to the mountains looking for a home. "We decided to make that 'right-angle' turn you were talking about and really start over in a new positive environment," Bob beamed. There was little available real estate in the Bradshaws at that time, so they decided to move to Phoenix until something opened up. Already owning an apartment house there gave them a place to stay and a project to work on.

I didn't talk to them again until November, when I called Bob to see if he'd be willing to sit in on a business planning session in Phoenix with several specialists in various business and psychic fields. When he arrived at the meeting, Mary wasn't with him. "She's really sick," he explained. "She's doing fantastically mentally, but an old kidney, liver, blood pressure problem keeps raising its negative head." Trenna and I both talked to her on the phone. The doctors didn't seem to be doing anything for her, so I gave her Norm Skeens' telephone number. "He might be able to help," I explained. "It doesn't sound like you have anything to lose by working with some psychic methodologies."

Norm Skeens is an ex-FBI man and presently a respected attorney in Glendale, Arizona, a suburb of Phoenix. He was a principal contact with law enforcement agencies seeking psychic help to solve criminal cases and in the past a contact for psychic healers. Many years ago Norm and I attended several hypnosis classes together as students. For years he has used his own money to finance psychic research, working with legitimate doctors and medical practitioners. They had accomplished many miraculous cures, yet the work has always been restricted because of a lack of funds. If the word "psychic" is attached to any research work, there is literally no major grant money available. On several occasions over the years I've sent to Norm extreme hardship cases which doctors had given up on hoping he could set up a contact with someone who could help them. I've always felt guilty about this because of the position it put him in.

Then during one of our Scottsdale seminars, it became obvious that a couple of the participants needed help beyond anything we could provide with hypnosis technology. They had come from thousands of miles away in hopes of finding answers to their problems in the seminar. Once again, feeling guilty, I gave them Norm's name and phone number.

A few days later he called me at our home. "I just wanted to say thank you for sending those people to us. I think we really helped them and one is coming back for a month's treatment," he explained.

"Thank you?" I responded. "I thought you'd be ready to read me the riot act!"

"No, no," he laughed, "we've been able to establish an organization called The Potential Research Foundation and opened the PRF Center of Alternative Therapy Development."

"Fantastic, Norm; tell me about it."

"Well, we have a good-sized building and a distinctive staff of two doctors, a Ph.D., three therapists, and a man who works with numerous methodologies, from psychic healing to naturopathic and physically manipulative techniques. Bio-feedback is another area and we're exploring many new concepts."

"So you are open to work with individual cases?" I asked.

"Certainly, and much of our present work concerns industrial accidents. These are people who have been injured on the job and have been referred to us by orthopedic surgeons. The insurance companies are paying these patients because they can't work; and our arrangement is that if we can't help them to return to work, there is no charge for our services. We now have a fifty-five percent success rate on cases which were considered beyond medical help."

"Could you give me a couple of quick case histories,

Norm, that would illustrate the type of problems you've helped solve?"

"We just finished working with a man who had been out of work for seventeen years. He had experienced multiple surgeries but couldn't walk. After one month of treatment, he is not only walking, but is back on the job. In another case we worked with a woman who had severe headaches for twenty-five years. Her husband is in the Air Force and she went through all the aerospace nuclear scans, etc., with no relief. She had one treatment a year ago and has had no headaches since. Naturally, we can't claim these kinds of results on all we've worked with, but new techniques seem to be opening up that are proving to be unbelievably effective."

In January, 1977, I called Mary. "How are you doing?"

"Oh fantastic, Dick," she responded. "Bob and I returned from Kansas City where we spent the holidays and nobody could believe it was us. Norm's clinic was so helpful to me that Bob decided to go in too. He's always so 'driving'; but with the help of biofeedback and the doctors there, he has mellowed out so much in the last couple of months that it's amazing. He's so much more at peace now."

"What about your own health problems, Mary? Were they able to help you in this area?"

"Oh yes, through stress elimination to begin with. They've also worked with reflexology and other techniques which have helped so much I don't believe it. Some of the things I do at home, I don't know why they work; but I can't argue with results. I feel good now."

CHAPTER 13

CASE HISTORY: CHARLOTTE— SEMINAR REGRESSION

Charlotte, a middle-aged, married woman, traveled two thousand miles to attend a five-day past life seminar in Scottsdale, Arizona. She was there in an attempt to understand and, hopefully, better her marital relationship. "My husband actually encouraged me to come," she explained. "This is the first time in twenty years of marriage that I've ever gone off to something alone." Her primary problems: Sexual incompatibility and lack of communication.

On the afternoon of the first day, I did a group regression session in which all participants were asked to seek a lifetime which they shared with someone now important in their present life. Once the induction was completed, they were asked to visualize the person in their mind, to mentally state the individual's name and attempt to capture their essence. Instructions were given to move backward in time to a prior life they have shared if indeed such a lifetime existed. Once the transfer was completed, many questions were asked and instructions were given to relive important situations.

Upon awakening the group of a hundred people lying on the floor and sitting in chairs in the Scottsdale Sheraton ballroom, I noticed Charlotte was crying softly to herself. Several people were gathered around attempting to comfort her. I explained that if she went deep enough to be upset I could easily remove the memories or impressions she'd received if she wanted me to. "Oh no," she explained. "I'll be fine in a minute. I wasn't getting any impressions at all until right before you brought us out of hypnosis. Then I received flashes of Rome . . . and they were taking away my babies. That's it, but it really upset me. I didn't receive anything else."

Since Charlotte was obviously a very good subject, I suggested that she might be one of those I used for individual directed demonstration sessions we would be doing during the evenings. This way, I could ask her questions and guide the past life tour. It would probably result in an understanding of the situations she had briefly tapped this afternoon.

She was apprehensive about it, so I told her to wait until the third evening. By then she would have much more understanding and could make a decision at the time. The night prior to the demonstrations, Charlotte used Higher-Self guide contact techniques she learned at the seminar before going to sleep. In the morning she told me, "I feel like the weight is falling away; I'm ready for that past life regression."

At 8:30 that evening she was a little scared but was in the hypnosis recliner preparing herself with a deep-breathing technique. The other participants were sitting on chairs or relaxing on pillows on the floor of the semidarkened room. My questions and Charlotte's answers would be amplified over the sound system so everyone could hear.

CHARLOTTE
Regression Session

Hypnosis induced and regression preparation completed, the subject was then instructed to go back to an important situation in the Roman lifetime she had briefly experienced in the previous group session:

Q. What do you see and what is happening at this time?

A. My little girl! (Her voice is cracking and she is attempting to hold back tears.) They're taking her away from me.

Q. Who is taking her away from you?

A. Widrough. (Phonetic spelling.) I'm on a bed of silk . . . it's a four-poster bed . . . (crying.) This is the third baby they've taken away . . . they can't do this . . . they . . . (More crying.)

Q. All right, now I want you to tell me about this situation without pain and without emotion. (Calming suggestions given.) Now why have they done this?

A. Because it wasn't a boy. That's all he wants from me . . . they will grow up to be warriors.

Q. You are speaking of your husband?

A. Yes. They can take over his leadership.

Q. They take your daughters away, and your husband is responsible for this?

A. Yes . . . he doesn't want me anyway . . . they tell me that the girls are deformed.

Q. I want you now to tell me your name.

A. Theo (Phonetic spelling.)

Q. Where do you live, Theo?

A. Rome.

Q. All right, I want you to let go of this now and move forward in time to another important situation that will transpire in the future. (Instructions given.) Tell me what is happening now.

A. I'm in the garden . . . it's quiet . . . this is my favorite place, but I came here because I know it is time for the boys' lessons.

Q. I take it these are your sons? How many do you have?

A. Four.

Q. Are you their teacher?

A. No, no . . . I don't want them to be taught! (The subject is becoming very upset and begins to shake. I motion for several in the group to come and place their hands on her.)

144

Q. Now I want you to stabilize . . . you are being given energy and I want you to accept it . . . it is being given freely and in love and you can now feel the warmth and calming energy coming in from the hands that are touching you. On the count of three, your body will return to normal. 1–2–3. Be at peace. Now what is it that you do not want your sons to be taught?

A. To fight. My husband insists they learn. My youngest is only seven, but he too must learn to fight.

Q. Tell me very truthfully exactly what you feel about your husband?

A. It has always been the same. After we were married, I knew . . . he can't show affection and . . . I need it so bad. So bad! I don't get to see my boys very much . . . they try to keep them away from me, but I know their schedule . . . when it is time for their training. I can't stand to be inside. (Strong emotion again.) They don't want me around.

Q. Do you still share physical relations with your husband?

A. Yes. (Crying—calming suggestions given.) I feel so cold, but I just keep thinking that if I'm with him, he'll show me some affection. (At this point, the subject became so upset that it was necessary to totally remove her from the prior life environment and return her to the present. In an attempt to examine the situation further, I moved her up into the Higher-Self superconscious mental levels.)

Q. All right now, Charlotte, you have transcended levels of consciousness and from the Higher-Self you will be able to look upon any aspect of your life objectively and without emotion. Your conscious mind is now connected; you have the expanded awareness of the superconscious, and all of the subconscious memories are right there at your mental fingertips. You have the ability to verbally communicate to me about the past life we were just examining, but you will now see it without reliving it. Now tell me of the outcome of the lifetime in Rome from the expanded overview you have from this perspective.

A. I'm happy we're dead!

Q. No, I want you to back up in time and tell me about what happened preceding the death experience.

A. I remained with my husband . . . he's forcing me to go with him . . . not because he wants me, and I don't know why because he can get sex from other women. I think it's because he doesn't want me around the children. He knows if he goes without me, I'll try to reach the children. There's two white horses, and we're going . . . I don't know where we're going; he hasn't told me. I don't want to go. He's angry! He never says anything; I don't know why he's angry. Oh, I think maybe it's because I didn't want to go with him. He's very powerful and nobody tells him no . . . except me.

Q. Is he ever physically violent with you?

A. He pushes me . . . but I push him back. We're leaving now . . . I don't like it; he is going so fast . . . he's going to go faster, because he's angry . . . we have to go up the side of the canyon . . . too fast . . . too fast . . . (Whispering now.) I can't tell him that because he'll just get madder . . . I've pushed him far enough . . . rock on the road . . . one of the wheels is hitting a rock . . . *We're going over the side of the cliff* . . . I'm in it!

Q. What about your husband, does he go over too?

A. No, he jumps free.

Q. And you were killed. Is this correct?

A. Yes.

Q. How old were you at this time?

A. Thirty-five.

Q. All right, I want you to completely let go of these impressions. While you remain in the Higher-Self realms of your own mind, I want to talk to you for awhile. I believe that what you shared with your husband in Rome, who is also your husband in your present life, is affecting today's relationship. Now from this transcended perspective, I want you to look down on your current life and talk to me about the sexual problems and your relationship in general. How do the karmic aspects relate from Roman life to this life?

A. It is the same basically. He tries so hard. He is always good to me sexually, but it's always sex. He never touches me unless it's a joke or . . . I shouldn't say that. It's not true. He does touch me sometimes. He tries . . . but I can feel . . . it's not just my problem; it's his problem too. It's not just me that has the problem. I can't stand him to touch me sometimes, and I can't hurt him either. He's trying so hard, but he doesn't feel it. (Strong emotion begins to surface.)

Q. All right, Charlotte, now we are trying to get to the bottom of this. There is no reason to carry these effects any longer. You have the power and ability to let go of the past and begin to create a new life in the present. By understanding the cause of the effects, you have the basis to let go and forget what has happened in the past. Now from the expanded awareness of the Higher-Self, I want you to speak up and tell me what you should be doing about your relationship—from this moment on. Now trust what comes into your mind, for your own Guides and Masters are right there with you, helping and directing you.

A. I should be accepting of what he has to offer. If I could do that, it would help him to channel his strong sex urge into a stronger life urge. We don't hurt each other from one life to another. We hurt each other from one year to another. It has been one year since he's run around on me. I try not to blame him, but he brought home V.D. (Strong emotion again.)

Q. Now relaxed and with peace and love—we are talking about this so you can begin to let go of it.

A. I punished him . . . I couldn't be warm with him . . . I got even colder. I just couldn't accept it, and I knew it was my fault, but I couldn't seem to change. Oh, we talked about it, but he lies . . .

147

even when he knows I know . . . he won't tell me the truth so we can bring it out in the open. Why? He won't talk about it. He won't talk about anything serious. But he is getting better lately.

Q. All right, what are you doing? What is your attitude towards him?

A. I'm trying. But when he goes out and doesn't tell me where he is going, then all the old doubts come back in.

Q. All right, now do you realize that the problems you have experienced are related to the past life we just examined and possibly many other prior incarnations the two of you have shared together?

A. Yes.

Q. Since you do realize this—that the past has created today—do you feel that you can let go of it? Unless you change your today, you are strengthening a negative bond that will carry forward into future incarnations. Now you are listening to my words from a transcended perspective. Can you let go of the past?

A. I can't do it . . . I can't do it with him.

Q. You can do anything you want to do.

A. If he wants to do it too, I can do it. I've got to have help. I need reassurance from him. I have no more will.

Q. Oh yes you do. You have the power and ability to change your own attitude. I agree that there is considerable karmic weight in the relationship you are now sharing, but you cannot expect someone else to change. As much as you would like to see this happen.

A. He is changing.

Q. This is beautiful, but you can't expect it to happen. It has to happen because he wants it to happen. But you can change yourself, and you can change your attitude about the situation. You can establish a detached perspective. Not that you will love him less, but you will love him for what he is, not what you would like him to be. Enjoy the moments—the

148

good moments; rise above the negative aspects through a detached perspective.

A. It's so hard. (Crying.)

Q. I realize it is hard, but you also realize from a karmic perspective that this is an opportunity and also a test. Your problems are related to the past; and unless you change the now, you will continue to live with these effects. You do not desire this, do you?

A. We have good times. We have many good times. I try to forget that he has had other women.

Q. There are good aspects to your relationship, so from this moment on, when negative thoughts—like the one you just described—come into your mind, I want you to brush them aside and cancel them out as we have discussed in this seminar. When the thoughts come in, you can dwell upon them and make yourself feel miserable or you can say, "I reject that thought and I send you love." Actually take a moment and send a thought of love to your husband. By dwelling upon negativity, you simply give it power, and from this moment on you are going to recognize and reject negative thoughts. Do you believe you can do this?

A. Yes.

Q. Can you send your husband love when such thoughts are recognized?

A. Yes.

Q. Then you can begin to turn your life around. You can create a new reality through these positive actions. You can create a new "you." Now you can't change him, but if he is reacting to a new you, he could very well be reacting in a new and more positive way.

A. I sure need a new me.

Q. Well, then it is certainly time to create you, isn't it? You have much strength, and you also now have much understanding. Do you believe me when I tell you that if you set your mind to it, you can create a new reality?

A. Yes.

149

Q. It would be foolish then to continue to accept yesterday's way of life when you don't have to. Now what I have been saying to you is being absorbed on conscious, subconscious and superconscious levels; and I want you to fully perceive and understand my words. I am now going to give you a trigger word, a conditioned response word which you will use whenever any form of negative thought comes into your mind, anytime you need to instantly recall the full understanding you have now achieved ... you will say the word "love." From this moment on, the word "love" is a trigger word which will instantly bring you back into high-level perspective. I leave you with this posthypnotic suggestion. The more you use it, the more effective it will become. Your karma is your responsibility; you can do nothing about another's. Don't look for change in your husband; don't expect it, and do not ask for it—approach him with love. (Additional suggestions and reinforcement given.)

(End of regression session.)

While Charlotte was relaxing in the hypnosis recliner, I talked to the group: "Thank you so much, those of you who laid your hands on Charlotte to give her energy. This is so real. There is no way for you to comprehend how effective that is until you've been in the position of receiving it. You were literally sharing your energy and she could feel it. (Charlotte nodded her head in agreement.) Believe me, you don't lose your energy when you give it in love. It comes back to you tenfold, and everyone benefits from it. (The group of six people who helped were now totally agreeing.) Now I want everyone in the room to understand that if this had been a privately directed therapy session, we'd have spent much more time and it would have probably included several hypnosis sessions. I'd have carried her back through additional past lives to show her that the position had

150

once been reversed. I'm sure Charlotte in previous lifetimes has given her present husband just as hard a time as he has given her—in other historic periods. These things are always a balance; but the thing to remember is, no matter what she found out about the past, the way to rise above it will still be the same. It's called *love*."

CHAPTER 14

CASE HISTORY:
CARL AND BETTYE—
CHAKRA LINK

Dallas, Texas—September 19, 1976: Carl and Bettye attended the seminar together and explained to me that they had been married for many years, but had spent the last five seeing various marriage counselors with very little result. Although they continued to remain together, both felt strong pressures to end the relationship.

Since they had both been receiving strong impressions during the two days of group regressions, I asked if they would like to attempt a "chakra link" during the Sunday evening demonstrations. This is a matter of having two people lie down side by side, holding hands, and my hypnotising them together. Next, the top five energy chakras are linked by having both individuals visualize an arch of the properly colored light connecting them. When this is successful, the results are often beyond everyone's highest expectations, for if the couple has shared a similar past lifetime, I can usually have them relive it together—each seeing the mental impressions from their own perspective. They literally reexperience yesterday's interaction, and there is normally little questioning as to whether or not the experience was based upon reality.

Carl and Bettye immediately volunteered, and that evening they were both lying on a roll-away bed in front of the speaker's platform. Ninety people quietly watched and listened.

CARL AND BETTYE
Regression Session

Hypnosis was induced, regression preparation completed, the chakra link established, and both subjects were moved into the Higher-Self mental levels. I then instructed: "I am calling in your own Guides and Masters to be with you during this session and I want you to call upon them to help you to use this time to its most beneficial advantage. You seek help and enlightenment, so call them in your mind now (a minute of silence). All right, your own Guides and Masters are now here with you; and you are working from a mental level way above your normal conscious abilities. If indeed you have shared a similar lifetime in another time and place, that would help to explain your present marital situation. I now want you to go backward in time to that lifetime. You will both perceive the same life and, Carl, I will be talking to you first. Bettye, I want you to follow along and let the impressions come into your mind as Carl is receiving them. (Instructions given.)

Q. What do you see or perceive at this time?
A. I'm on a . . . floor . . . I'm on a dirt floor . . . my mother's there.
Q. How old are you at this time?
A. About a year . . . I can barely walk. I want her to . . . love me . . . to pick me up. But she's too busy.
Q. What else is happening?
A. She's cooking.
Q. All right, I now want you to move forward in time a little ways until something important happens. (Instructions given.) What is happening now?
A. It's the same cabin . . . in the woods, and I just

153

killed a deer. I'm about twelve and I brought it in. We needed the meat.

Q. Does your family live in the cabin?

A. Just my mother. I don't remember a father.

Q. Is your mother happy that you got the deer?

A. No, she wants to know why I took so long.

Q. Tell me about the relationship you now share with your mother at the age of twelve.

A. I want her to be happy. I want her to love me, but there is nothing I can do that is right.

Q. You do not feel that she loves you?

A. No.

Q. What is your name?

A. Jeremiah.

Q. Let's move forward in time once again, Jeremiah, until something important happens. (Instructions given.)

A. I'm looking over a meadow. There's where we used to live.

Q. How old are you now?

A. Fifteen . . . but we don't live there any more.

Q. What happened or changed in the last three years?

A. The log cabin's fallen down. Mother's gone . . . she died one winter.

Q. Whom do you live with now?

A. I'm by myself; I live in the woods.

Q. All right, I now want you to let go of these impressions and move back into the Higher-Self mental levels. (Instructions given.) Now trust your mind, Carl, and explain to me how the situations you just experienced relate to your present life.

A. Bettye was my mother in that lifetime.

Q. All right, Carl, I now want you to remain silent and simply flow along with Bettye as I talk to her for awhile. Bettye, can you tell me if you were perceiving the visual impressions as Carl was receiving them?

A. Yes . . . I saw the child on the dirt floor. I saw what the child had on. I saw the calico dress the mother was wearing . . . it was brown with pink flowers . . . little tiny pink flowers, and she wore

154

an apron. Her hair was parted back in the middle—
pulled back. She had a stern face.

Q. Do you personally relate to this? Was there a soul
level of identification? . . . Were you this woman?

A. Yes . . . but I cannot be pleased.

Q. All right, Bettye, I know there is much more to
this, so I want you now to maneuver in time. Allow
impressions to come into your mind that will help
to further establish the background for the relationship that you and Carl now share. (Instructions given.)

READER'S NOTE: To fully comprehend what follows, it is important to understand that Bettye
now moves forward in time to her next incarnation. Almost immediately following her death as
Carl's mother, she was reborn in the same lo-
cality. When she grows up, she marries Carl
(Jeremiah), who is fourteen or fifteen years older
than she. It was also later explained that she
reincarnated to be her own son's wife because
she didn't like the karmic implications and was
anxious to work them out.

Q. What do you see and what is happening at this
time?

A. I'm confused . . . I'm getting two images.

Q. The most important image will come in stronger,
in sharp focus; and the other will dissipate on the
count of three. 1-2-3. All right, now speak up and
tell me what you perceive.

A. I'm in a cabin . . . it's clean. The whole cabin is
clean and neat and polished and beautiful. It is the
prettiest cabin I've ever seen. It even has windows.

Q. What else can you tell me?

A. I am young and pretty and I smell good. My love
is coming, but I don't want him to come now.

Q. Why not?

A. Jeremiah is coming home from hunting.

Q. Who is Jeremiah?

A. He's my husband. Jeremiah is a violent man, and I

155

don't want him to see Micah. Micah is my love, but he's just a friendly person now.

Q. Is Micah your lover?

A. No, not sexually, he just brings me flowers. We talk and we walk by the river. I came here with Jeremiah. He brought me from the home and he built me this beautiful cabin. It's right on the bank of the river . . . deep in the woods.

Q. Can you tell me the name of the river?

A. Susquehanna. [NOTE: The Susquehanna River is the largest river in Pennsylvania, New York, and Maryland, ending in Chesapeake Bay. It is a shallow rapid stream that becomes a raging torrent in late winter. Bettye had never consciously heard of this river.]

Q. What is happening now?

A. Micah is standing in the doorway, talking to me, and Jeremiah comes home. He is angry because of his violence. He is taking all of my belongings . . . he won't listen to me . . . he's taking all of my belongings and throwing them outside. *He's locking the door!* I must go away with Micah.

Q. Tell me more.

A. I love Micah, but he's just a trapper. He doesn't have any security for me. I never had any before Jeremiah.

Q. Let's move forward in time a ways. I want to know how this evolves. (Instructions given.)

A. Micah and I don't get along at all. I need security and he cannot provide that. Love is not enough for me. I'm pregnant and Micah disappeared. He left me in this horrible lean-to kind of a cabin and it's cold . . . and I'm pregnant. I want to go back to Jeremiah.

Q. Is that a consideration?

A. It's the only way.

Q. All right, if you do indeed attempt to reestablish the ties with Jeremiah, I want you to move forward in time to see what unfolds. (Instructions given.)

A. I go back to Jeremiah and I crawl on my knees and tell him I'm sorry and he throws me out.

I'm lying there on the banks of the river and I look at the water and it's dark and cold and swirling and I see that that's my only way out, I start to go into the water and something stops me. I can't because of my baby . . . the baby is very important. Jeremiah really loves me, but his pride is in the way. I must go back to Jeremiah and take whatever it is that he hands out.

Q. Let's move forward again in time. (Instructions given.)

A. Jeremiah still slaps me around and beats me once in awhile, but it doesn't hurt that much . . . and I know he does love me. I'm angry with him for doing that. I hate his pride. But the child is special. It's a boy and has black hair and big, beautiful blue eyes. And he looks at me and he knows . . . he just knows . . . knows what I go through for him. His knowing makes it easier for me. But I dread when Jeremiah comes home at night, because I don't know what he's going to do.

Q. How much time has elapsed since you returned to Jeremiah?

A. Two . . . three years.

Q. And he still carries the animosity?

A. Yes.

Q. Tell me about your child?

A. I feel great, great love. I'm a very good mother. We go for picnics together in the meadow . . . and we throw rocks in the river . . . and we make mud pies on the bank. His name is Joseph. He knows that Jeremiah really loves him. He . . . he sleeps in the loft and when Jeremiah loses his temper with me, he cries himself to sleep. But yet he seems to understand. He doesn't hold any grudges against Jeremiah. It's all right because he knows that I don't hurt.

Q. All right, let's move forward in time quite a ways now . . . until something very important transpires. (Instructions given.)

A. Joseph is a very tall, handsome young man and he is going away to school; I taught him all I knew.

157

They taught us at the home to write and read; and I taught him in the dirt how to write. The circuit rider also helped to teach him how to read. He is going away to school because he's very smart and he's very special. I'm so proud of him.

Q. What about Jeremiah? Where is he now?

A. He's older. He was always older than I. He's standing back watching with great pride. Joseph goes off.

Q. All right. I now want you to come back to the present time and you'll remain in a deep hypnotic sleep, in the Higher-Self realms of your own mind. (Instructions given.) Can you now tell me, Bettye, how this lifetime relates to your present life?

A. Carl was Jeremiah. I don't know who Micah was. My son in that life is now my youngest son.

Q. A psychic connection now exists between the two of you. You both have much knowledge about your own past and I want any information that you can supply me with about your relationship to simply flow out now. Bettye, I want you to talk to me first.

A. I can't trust him. He tells me he loves me but I can't trust him. He used to beat me up and say he loved me . . . and I'm getting revenge on him . . . for beating me up and throwing me out and not listening to me and not hearing me. *I don't want to do that* . . . that's not like me!

Q. No, you've been influenced very strongly by something that happened in a prior lifetime and there is absolutely no need to carry this effect forward. Now you mentioned sexual problems to me prior to this evening's sessions. How is your lack of trust manifesting as these problems? I want you to face it. I want you to look at it, and then you can let go of it. Talk to me about this.

A. I cannot give myself to a man who might hurt me. He's hurt me in this life, but he doesn't do that any more.

Q. You've both hurt each other in this life.

A. Yes . . . we both want to stop. I trust others . . . I want so much to trust him.

Q. I feel that you have now made a major break-through in understanding why you do not trust Carl. Carl should also have understanding as to why he feels rejected by you. You are both carrying negativity related to the past. You've come back together once again in an attempt to rise above these effects. You are here to learn to perfect your love; and through wisdom, to erase your karma. I believe you have some of this wisdom now . . . and in knowing the cause, you should be able to use the wisdom to let go. There is no longer any need to carry this forward. We have already talked much in this seminar about perfecting love and you can use this knowledge to the betterment of your relationship. (Additional suggestions given.) Do you understand?

Bettye. Oh, yes!

Carl. Yes.

Q. All right, before I begin to speak with Carl, is there any additional knowledge, Bettye, that you can provide? Is there any knowledge available from your own Guides and Masters? Listen quietly for a moment to what they are saying to you; and if you can share it, I would like you to do so.

A. Carl and I are to progress together in this life . . . to move up to level of communicating that nothing can touch.

Q. Thank you, Bettye. You have one methodology right now—a very effective one. You may choose others over this one, but this is a beginning of communications. You can both return to this mental level, and you can do it together through the techniques you have learned. If you both sincerely, consciously, desire to rise above these effects, you can easily do so. You can begin to share a beautiful relationship. Begin to live for "now." Now is all that exists. By understanding the past, you can let go of the past. I am now going to talk to Carl for awhile. Carl, if you are receiving more information from your own Guides and Masters, or if you can elaborate upon Bettye's experiences, I would like you to do so.

A. When she left, I was mad. I didn't think she would go. I waited for her. I never found her.

Q. What are you speaking of now?

A. When she left with Micah. I knew she'd come back. Micah was a poet. Poets don't live in the woods very long. I was wrong. When I threw her out . . . I beat her because I hated myself.

Q. Yes?

A. So, in this life I've got to keep trying.

Q. I want you both to understand that there is no guilt on one side more than on the other. There is no guilt at all. There is no blame. We could continue with this session all night and into the days that follow, probably finding lifetime after lifetime in which the balance between you would swing back and forth. I do not think that is necessary. In one case we have a child rejected by the mother. In another, the husband rejects the wife. Now you can go on with this self-punishment game if you want to, but I think you both know better than that now.

A. I'm through with this shit.

(End of regression session.)

Several months after the chakra-link regression I contacted Carl and Bettye to ask how they were doing. She sent me a letter filled with interesting details and additional verifications. In regard to their life together, she had this, in part, to say:

> The regression did some releasing and permission-giving; and we both needed that very much; however, we still know that we have a lot of work ahead of us. It is like an architect having a fantastic vision about a building he is to create. The difference is between the glories of the vision and the everyday stacking of one brick on top of

another. Well, I have come down off of the high of the vision and have become an ordinary hod-carrying, mortar-slapping, bricklayer. And completion is a long way up from the foundation. But at times, I still become the visionary architect; and the dreams I dream are still beautiful . . . and they keep me going.

CHAPTER 15

LOVE, PEACE
AND PROBLEMS

"Maybe I should just get a divorce?" she said, looking to me for an answer.

"Maybe," I replied.

"Well, we just can't seem to get along at all!" Feigned emotions were now beginning to surface. "I've heard you say that sometimes the only way to be responsible to yourself was to remove yourself from the environment you find yourself within?"

"I believe that's true, Nancy," I responded. "But don't use my words as a rationale to divorce your husband."

"I've tried; believe me I've tried, but he just won't make any efforts at all."

"What kind of efforts do you expect him to make?" I asked.

"Well . . . to be nicer to me. I wish he wouldn't go out with the guys all the time. He's not tender during sex anymore either!" she stated, as if that were the ultimate proof.

"Then you want him to change, to be the way you want him to be?"

"Ah . . . no, I really don't want him to change, but I wish he'd just want to be that way."

"Then you'd be happy?"

"Yes."

"What does he feel about you? Would he like to see you change in some way?"

"Well . . . yes, but the things that bug him are so dumb. I think we'd both be happier with other people!"

"For awhile probably," I replied. "You're already involved with someone else, aren't you?"

"Ah, yes, but how'd you know that?"

"A little bird told me. You've already made your decision and now you're simply looking for reinforcement wherever you can find it."

"Well, you say love and peace are the pathway to harmony," she said with anger beginning to show in her voice. "I'm in love with Jack and I feel peaceful when I'm with him. I certainly can't say that about my husband!"

This conversation was real, but it is simply a tape recording of hundreds of variations we've heard. People relate words like "love" and "peace" on a superficial level. In this case love with Jack simply meant that Jack was being what she wanted him to be; thus she was not threatened. Peace, by her interpretation, was the result of having things her way. Jack's attentiveness and willingness to fit her mold supported her own insecurity. The chances of the situation remaining stable over a period of time are obviously slight.

Close to our home in the mountains is a special place where I go and talk to the mountain. Maybe I'm simply talking to myself or an alternate aspect of myself, but the answers come in and I write them down. As I evolve in my own metaphysical growth, I find myself moving more and more into the basic American Indian belief system. My own Guides are Indians, as is my primary reincarnational lineage, so this may be the reason much of my communications from the unseen relates so strongly to this lifestyle. Many of these "talks" will be included in a new poetry book I recently finished, called, *Spirit Mountain Speak to Me*.* Because they are such simplified, di-

---

* Valley of the Sun Publishing Co.

rect statements about the real meaning of love, marriage and peace, I am including a few of them here:

> Spirit Mountain
>   speak to me
>   of the secrets
>   you retain

> The secrets lie
>   in feelings that
>   your heart can
>   well explain . . .

>   so remain with
>   me in silence
>   seeking wisdom
>   in the ways
>   of long forgotten
>   Indians
>   who once came
>   here to pray.

LOVE: "Love with all of its subtleties and intensities is the reason you walk on the earth mother. Love is the absence of fear. You exist for love and through love you grow. Accept it freely, but hold it with an open hand. Give it freely, but without expectation of return. Surround yourself with love, and in so doing, it will expand and grow—filling the seasons of your life with the power of all powers."

MARRIAGE: "Marriage is an alliance of compatible energies for the creation of harmonious energy, and in harmony lie fulfillment and unity. Protect marriage with freedom and the space to grow individually. Shield marriage with a united offensive in the face of adversity. Strengthen marriage with a selfless attitude. When you have evolved beyond expectation and learned to find joy in what is bestowed, your marriage will have matured and will be secured. It will be the foundation of your dreams and the sunshine of your soul."

PEACE: "Peace is an internal emotion achieved through self-satisfaction and the elimination of fear from your thoughts. Many in harmonious environments know little of peace. Many in the mud of battlefields know much of peace. Seek it in your attitude towards life and your acceptance of yourself. When combined with love, it is the power of the universe."

FEAR: "Fear is the only problem that exists in the mind of man. It is the basis of all negative manifestation. Guilt, greed, possessiveness, insecurity, frustration, tension, anxiety, indifference and boredom are all emotions rooted in fear. They are the cause of all conflicts and confrontations; and as surely as fear is the problem, *love* is the answer."

THE MEANING OF LIFE: "Life itself is the meaning of life; and in listening to the laughter of a child, you will understand. When you learn to find merit in the darkest of hours and pleasure in the simplicity of a wild flower, you will understand. Do not search for the meaning of life in others, but rather in your own small joys, for they are the key to understanding. Examine them and expand upon them. When you have found satisfaction in the pursuit of your goals—not in their accomplishment—you will understand."

LOST LOVE: "Love is never lost; for once love is, it is always. There are times when the path must fork; but when it does, there is a reason beyond that of your eyes. Yesterday's harmony is not gone; but like the rain, has been absorbed to appear once more as new growth and in time will flower in the sun. Now is the time to walk your own path with an open heart. Let the visions of new desires dance freely in your mind, for in them lies the power to create springtime in the moon of the falling leaves."

DESTINY: "Destiny is clay in your hands. You are the sculptor—the creator. Work your dreams into tangible forms and creations of beauty. Use your imaginings like a true craftsman; for all thoughts, given energy, will manifest in some form. As the decisive artist, you have the ability to take full control of destiny; but through indecision, destiny has the ability to take full control of you. Your only limitation is your own creativity."

PROBLEMS: "When your mind is troubled, use what energy you have for centering and the problems will solve themselves. Do not solicit external crutches, but instead seek the inner wisdom which lies latent in the very essence of your being. Begin your search for peace in the place you find peace, for there is an environment you have experienced which is more compatible with your energy than any other. Listen in silence to the sound of silence, and your heart will speak to you with a voice you cannot ignore. Make your decisions and stand upon them, for in commitment there is strength. Walk in freedom without looking behind you, and without guilt—the most foolish of emotions. Your only problems are those you yourself accept.

> The power is with you—use it.
> The wisdom is in you—employ it.
> The unity surrounds you—accept it.
> Love is the answer—give it."

CHAPTER 16

CASE HISTORY:
BEN AND CHRISTINA

We met Ben and Christina Goddard through a unique set of circumstances, which, in retrospect, was certainly maneuvered by an unseen plan. They are among the few people I can truly claim I "already knew" the moment we shook hands. Sitting over coffee in a Prescott diner, we talked about metaphysics and hypnotic regression. They explained they were passing through town on their way to Santa Fe, New Mexico, where one of their two advertising agencies was located. For nearly two years they'd been organizing and managing primary election compaigns for a little-known political candidate named Jimmy Carter. All activities in the thirteen Western states and the crucial New Hampshire primary were handled by their agency.

Carter had received the Democratic party nomination, and the job they'd contracted to do was completed. "We're tired," Christina said. "We were married just before accepting the Carter assignment, and we've been going night and day ever since. We don't even know what it will be like to live under normal conditions."

The Goddards had experienced their fill of the business world and were seeking to withdraw into a more quiet life of writing and free-lance assignments. "We'd like to move out into the country somewhere," Ben explained. "On our way to Santa Fe we're going to look at Flagstaff and some other out of the way places as considerations for a new home. Prescott itself is pretty interesting as a matter of fact."

Ben and Christina had each been married previously and each had a son. Both boys were traveling with them at the time, and all were staying at a local motel. I invited them out to stay with us at our home in the mountains for the couple of days they would be in town.

"Now this is the sort of environment we could be happy in!" Christina exclaimed upon their Sunday afternoon arrival. The midsummer temperature in the Bradshaws is about 80° and most people fall in love with the pine trees and mountain creeks in that section of national forest, which is at 6,500 feet elevation.

The Goddards had read *You Were Born Again to Be Together* and were interested in reincarnation and the concept of past life regression. I volunteered to do a couple of regression sessions, and that evening we went out to the studio to begin. Christina decided to go first.

CHRISTINA
Regression Session

Hypnosis induced, spiritual protection incorporated and the regression preparation was completed. The following instructions were then given: "If you and your present husband Ben have been together in a previous lifetime . . . in another time and another place, I now want you to go backward in time to a situation that transpired in this other historic period. If you have not been together before, you will be able to speak up and tell me on the completion of the count. If you have been together in more than one previous incarnation, your own subconscious mind will choose a lifetime that would be desirable to reexamine at this time." (Instructions given.)

Q. Can you speak up now and tell me what you see, or feel, and what you are doing at this time?

A. I'm female, dressed in white . . . off white . . . homespun . . . There's a belt . . . a dark belt . . . it's loose fit. My shoes are woven . . . there is some kind of cross lacing. My hair is short . . . and I'm just standing outside. There are dark mountains way off in the distance. No . . . I think I'm a boy not a girl . . . the hair is almost a bowl cut . . . it's brown . . . I feel like I'm all alone in the middle of the valley . . . the dawn's coming.

Q. How old are you at this time?

A. Fifteen.

Q. All right, I want you to let go of this and move forward in time to an important situation that will transpire in your future. (Instructions given.) Tell me what is happening now.

A. I'm sitting in a chair . . . a large chair . . . all in white . . . I feel a lot of people around me . . . but I can't seem to see them. I don't believe it is me in the chair. . . . There's a woman in the chair . . . it isn't me. I feel a connection with her though. (Christina is now confused about what she is receiving, so she is given the freedom to simply allow impressions to flow in and to talk about them as they occur.) I see a long road that goes forever, and there's grass on both sides . . . and the sky is huge. I'm walking. . . . Everything is a very strange way of perceiving . . . like I'm blind . . . I feel I'm blind. I feel alone. There is heat inside my body. I saw a building, but it went from pillars to having a point on the top. Can't seem to set myself in . . . I don't know . . .

Q. You do have the ability to totally relive an important event that transpired in this lifetime we are now examining. (Special instructions given in an attempt to clear up the impression.) Now tell me what is happening.

A. It's a dark hole, but it's square . . . I'm blocking it, I know I'm blocking it, I'm hearing the words that say, no you can't see it, you can't do it.

Q. I know you're blocking it, but you do have the power and ability to experience it and thus understand it. Tell me about the black hole.

A. It's dark . . . it's wide open . . . in the middle of nothing . . . I think if you walked into it you'd be gone.

Q. If something is going to transpire regarding this hole, I want you to move to that time.

A. There's no fear . . . but my eyes feel like they've been gouged out. I'm sealed in, or something . . . I can feel the wall . . . it's square, and I can feel where the four sides end . . .

Q. (Christina was obviously blocking reliving the experience, so I now moved her into the Higher-Self levels of her mind, transcending levels of consciousness so she could look down upon this previous lifetime as an observer.) All right, now from this perspective I want you to tell me about this life.

A. There is part of me in both places . . . I feel above yet I'm still there . . . I feel like I'm slowly being crushed . . . I don't understand it . . . the more I try to understand, the more I feel as if I'm being blocked . . . I want to stop the block . . . I can feel this sensation of being crushed throughout my whole body . . . I'm developing a cold sweat . . . I don't understand. (At this point, since Christina was blocking the impressions and was beginning to feel quite uncomfortable, I decided to bring her out of the trance.)

(End of session.)

Upon awakening she felt all the more confused. "The impressions that were coming in were very vivid," she explained, "but everything was fuzzy and I couldn't relate it all. The emotions and effects were certainly vivid!"

It was now Ben's turn to regress, so he made himself comfortable in the chair and began to breathe deeply.

BEN
Regression Session

I did not initially instruct him to go to a lifetime in which he and Christina had been together in a previous period. He was told: "Choose a lifetime that would be of value for you to relive at this time." The result was a primitive lifetime that proved extremely interesting, with him reexperiencing the highlights of his death in a battle with another tribe.

Ben was now moved into the Higher-Self levels of his own mind and from this all-knowing perspective I asked, "Can you tell me about Christina's experience in the lifetime she was blocking out earlier? A lifetime in which the two of you were together?"

A. She rejected the priestess. The priestess is a fat ugly woman and very powerful. She has life and death powers, and she gathers around her young boys. She uses them for her own personal pleasure. They perform many sex acts with her . . . that is her satisfaction. One boy fell in love with a girl. He was a very beautiful boy and she hated him for it, so she destroyed him. She made him watch the disembowelment of the girl, and then she put out his eyes and threw him in a pit and crushed him with a large stone.

Q. How are you involved in this situation?

A. I don't know . . . I'm seeing it as an observer . . . but I feel a connection, an attachment.

Q. (Several additional questions were asked here in an attempt to allow the full information to channel through. Since he was obviously blocking, I changed the subject to that of a baby that Christina had miscarried several months earlier. She was concerned about this and and I had planned to question

171

her about it, but did not get the chance.) Can you tell me anything about the baby you lost and how this relates to you karmically?

A. I believe the baby is connected to the lifetime of the priestess. The girl who was killed by the priestess was pregnant by the boy. That's why the priestess killed them both . . . the boy is her property. I see step pyramids . . . long, long ago. The priestess wears white robes . . . she's a very large, huge woman. She has black hair. There's some embroidery on the robe . . . on the front. She sits on a raised platform in a chair, a gold chair, and there are eagles on the tops of the back, and she is on a raised platform at the base of the pyramid . . . and people are sacrificed on the top of the pyramid.

Q. All right, I now want you to place yourself into this lifetime. How do you relate to the activities you've observed? Who are you?

A. I don't want to be the priestess!

Q. Trust your mind; that may not be the situation at all.

A. I'm afraid it is. My body feels fat. Everything is swimming. I'm going in and out of it. There's a belt of some kind . . . a black belt . . . something hanging from it. When I get too close it feels very uncomfortable. Light is coming in . . . light blue and sky . . . it's a different place I think. There are white pillars, white marble pillars. It's Greece . . . there is a cliff and the ocean is down below.

Q. (Fully realizing that Ben's subconscious mind had switched to another lifetime in an attempt to avoid further painful observations, I simply let him flow with the experience.) Is this a lifetime in which you and Christina were together?

A. Yes . . . I see a boy in a white, loose-fitting gown, with dark hair. He has a flute. Animals . . . sheep . . . it's very green, very pretty. There doesn't seem to be anything special about this . . . it's just a peaceful place.

Q. All right, we're going to let go of this for a moment

172

and I now want to know if there are other lifetimes that you and Christina have shared? You are in the higher levels of your own mind and all of the subconscious memories are right there at your mental fingertips.

A. England . . . heavy wool dark clothes . . . it's cold. There are buildings . . . old buildings . . . 1700's. We're together and there's a carriage. We're getting into a black carriage. We look so young. We're children together. Yes, we're brother and sister . . . and there's our mother. She's a very pretty lady and she is getting into the carriage too and she is wearing very dark clothes. Someone has just died. Oh . . . our father died and we're going to the funeral.

Q. All right, let's let go of this and see if there is another life the two of you have shared.

A. Ireland. Yes, Ireland. A white-ruffled, lacy kind of shirt with a tie and drawstring brown pants with a belt and he has light blond hair and freckles. There is a girl in a green dress. I see a road, and there is a wooden fence and trees. There is something wrong. I see a rusted oblong thing on his head. It seems to be a wound, or a sore, and she is trying to treat it. She is taking care of me.

Q. Let's move forward in time a little ways and see what else transpires.

A. I died from this. She tried very hard. We're in a cottage. It's a very small cottage of stone and she is washing me and trying to nurse me back to health. She loves me very much, and is very sad when I die, but I seem quite peaceful, for I'm still there with her and we'll be together again.

Q. All right, I now want you to pull the memories from your superconscious mind, or from Christina's subconscious mind, in regard to a fear we discussed earlier. Christina said before her regression that she has always feared to be hurt, especially around her mouth and legs. She has nothing to base this upon from her present life, so if you can provide

173

any information as to the cause of this fear I would like you to do so.

A. This relates to the pit. It was a very evil thing . . . very evil . . . because he is blind, his eyes have been put out and he is in the pit and he knows what is going to happen. There is a huge block that is lowered into the pit and comes down, slowly, slowly, slowly and crushes him. It is very painful and the basis of the fear.

Q. I know you may have many questions in your own mind and from this Higher-Self level you can ask them and receive answers. If you would care to verbalize any information, you are now free to do so.

A. I have a hard time getting away from the priestess . . . I keep wanting to go back there, but it feels very uncomfortable, because I know that I could have stopped that. I was the priestess. I hated him . . . he betrayed me.

Q. Now so you will fully understand the balancing aspects involved here, I know that something transpired in a different lifetime that caused you, the priestess, to perpetrate this act. Over the centuries your love has grown and developed, but way, way back there in time there is another lifetime in which the two of you probably were in a similar but reversed situation. If so, I want you now to allow memories of such a situation to flow into your mind. (Instructions given.)

A. Something on my legs . . . I'm getting flashes but it's not very comfortable I'll tell you. Sword . . . something with a sword . . . ah . . . I'm a soldier wearing a breastplate of armor. It's round, with hard leather . . . and brass. I've been cut. My body's been cut in two right at my genitals right across my legs . . . my lower body has almost been severed. He did that! Blond soldier . . . he was Christina.

Q. All right, now I want you to fully understand that we all evolve through situations that are not particularly desirable when viewed from our

174

present perspective, but this is an evolutive situation for our own growth. You and Christina have given each other very hard times at different points in history, but through the lifetimes we've touched, and there are probably many more, you are perfecting love. That is the reason you are now back together. It is time to let go of the past and of all fears that might have affected you in the past. By understanding the past you can let go of the past. It is now time to perfect the love the two of you share.

(End of regression session.)

Ben later admitted that maybe he'd learned more than he really needed to know, but the regressions did help to explain particular aspects of their relationship.

Later that summer the Goddards moved to Prescott and rented a home in the mountains a few miles from us. They spend much of their time flying in and out of larger cities to produce commercials and carry on their consulting services, but feel the extra effort is worth it to live in a quiet mountain environment.

We have worked with them on our own seminars and Christina is now talking quite a bit about a creative concept of her own—to produce another Goddard.

CHAPTER 17

MY OWN CASE HISTORY:
THE ED MORRELL STORY

Objectivity is our primary consideration in research-ing past life case histories, and in this case, I've at-tempted to be particularly unbiased, for it involves me. I didn't search out the information. It came in the back door and for over a year and a half additional data has continued to appear. The cross-verifications and confirmations have now gone beyond the possibil-ity of coincidence. Regressive hypnosis was only used as one of the final confirmations.

August, 1975: Every Tuesday and Thursday morn-ing, over a period of several months, I met with David Chethlahe Paladin in his studio for taped interview sessions. As I've previously written, David has the ability to allow several discarnates to speak through him, and the reason for the biweekly meetings was to gather future book material. Kandy was speaking about a personal friend of David's and how their present relationship had manifested in other historic periods. In an attempt to clarify a point, I mentioned the name of a close friend of mine who is a country music singer-songwriter. "Can you tell me of other lives he and I have shared, Kandy?"

"Visualize him in your mind for a moment," Kandy replied in his thick Russian-accented English voice. "Ah, yes, the two of you have been together several times." He went on to explain the basic details of a couple of lifetimes. They made sense and tended to explain some underlying aspects of our friendship. Then he continued: "From your perspective, you might not agree, but you also owe him a great deal. He was one of those who was responsible for your being sent to prison, but because of this, you met Jack London, and it had a strong influence on your becoming a writer."

I questioned Kandy no more about it at the time, but later asked a writer friend of mine if London had ever been in prison. "Once for lobster poaching and another time for vagrancy," he told me. That was the extent of my follow-up. It was an interesting bit of information, but only one of hundreds of interesting things we were investigating at the time. As a young boy I'd read many of London's outdoor books, but that was the extent of my identification with the man. The information was more or less forgotten until almost a year later.

July, 1976: Trenna and I were sitting on our front porch visiting with author Richard Bach. "By the way, Dick, have you ever read a book of Jack London's called *The Star Rover?* It's about reincarnation and astral projection . . . about a man in prison."

Trenna and I looked at each other. "Why are you asking me that out of the clear blue sky, Richard?"

"I don't know," he responded. "It just came in. You really should read it, though. It's quite hard to find because it was printed shortly after the turn of the century and was never one of London's more popular books. I have a copy; and if you can't find one, I could Xerox it for you."

August, 1976: It was a house guest weekend at our Prescott home. Joanne Ordean, a long-time friend who is very interested in metaphysics, had come over from California, and Ben and Christina Goddard, whose case history I wrote about in the previous chapter, had just finished their organizational assignment on the Jimmy Carter presidential campaign in the western

177

part of the country. They were now in Prescott to find a home.

We decided to invite David and Lynda Paladin over for a Sunday brunch, wanting everyone to meet. A couple of hours into the general conversation, I recalled Bach's words about Jack London's book. I addressed myself to David. "Kandy, you told me something about a year ago that I'd like to ask you some more about if you don't mind?" David's eyes seemed to change—the pupils dilated and an alien intensity became quite obvious.

"Of course," replied the familiar voice of my Russian friend.

"Well, you told me I was in prison in my last incarnation, and through this I met Jack London and it influenced my writing career."

"Remember there is no time, so although you think of it as your last life, it is still transpiring. Yes, you were in prison, but they couldn't keep you there . . . you kept astral-projecting out. They could imprison your body, but not your mind or spirit. You will soon come to know much more of this."

A discussion of the known facts followed, and Joanne said that she was sure she could find *The Star Rover* for me in Los Angeles. I still wasn't all that intrigued with the case, but I told her if she could without much trouble, I'd appreciate it.

It was a warm, enjoyable day, with good friends and stimulating conversation. As usual, Kandy ate all of David's desserts. When David allows the discarnates to speak through him, he retains little conscious knowledge of what has transpired during the period he has transcended consciousness. Kandy has a knack of getting into the discussions at dessert time. When David came back in, he looked at his empty plate and asked, "It looks like it must have been good. What did I have?"

The Paladins left in the early afternoon. Then the rest of us went down to a large pool on a nearby creek for a swim. That evening we gathered around the fireplace in the living room. Christina demonstrated a

178

special massage technique she had learned as a new-age seminar instructor. I was the recipient of the massage, and it left me feeling extremely relaxed and a little lightheaded.

Several minutes later I still felt spaced out as I sorted through a stack of record albums to choose something to put on the stereo. What appeared to be a small, brightly colored snowflake was superimposed on a record jacket. I brushed at it and then realized that it was my eyes. My first thought was that I'd been staring at a bright light and the radiating glow was the natural illusion created by such action. Yet, the only light in the room was a kerosene lamp behind me and a low-watt bulb in a lamp in the other corner of the room.

A few blinks later, I realized it was growing larger. What started out as a quarter-inch snowflake was now at least an inch and continuing to grow. I closed my eyes tightly—it was just as clear and growing larger by the minute. By the time it was about six inches, I was getting concerned that either my eyes or mind were going, and I moved over to the couch and lay down. Trenna immediately moved to my side. "Richard, what's wrong?" she whispered.

"I don't know, but from my perspective we're about to get one hell of a colored snowstorm." I explained what was happening and by now it was a good eighteen inches and growing, but it was big enough to see details. The image wasn't a circle, but was a giant "C." Instead of a snowflake it was like a stained glass design, the basic Indian step design in bright green, red, blue and yellow. Trenna now had her hand on my forehead, but the design was superimposed right over her arm. It continued to grow until it was almost beyond my vision, but as the last of it passed the left side of my head, it began to swirl and sparkle like a blue ballroom chandelier. Then it turned dazzling white and either entered right behind my left ear or moved beyond me. Ten or twelve minutes had passed from the time it appeared.

There was an interesting discussion that followed

179

regarding the possibilities. I felt fine, but couldn't relate it to anything. "I don't know what the hell it was, so if it went inside, I'm not so sure I like it," was my only conclusion.

The next day I called David and told him about the experience. "As you know, David, we have nothing to do with any kind of dope. I'd had a beer during the evening but that was it. What do you make of it?"

"I don't know," he told me. "I've had light experiences, and I've heard of somewhat similar forms of visions, but I'm afraid I just don't know."

A few days later we were doing a seminar in Scottsdale. Kingdon Brown was one of our guest speakers, and I told him of the experience while we were sitting visiting in the motel room waiting to go on stage.

"I don't know," he told me. "That's a strange one. I'm not receiving any input, but I'd be glad to work on it if you'd like."

"No, don't bother, Kingdon; it's not that important." But evidently it was important, for I couldn't get it out of my mind. One afternoon about a week after the experience I was alone in the house, and found myself thinking about it again. At this point I decided to find my own answers, so I used Higher-Self hypnosis as my psychic methodology. From a deep trance I sent out the thought: "All right, you guys . . . what was the deal on the big, pretty 'C' and where did it go?"

An inner voice came back as strong as I've ever heard it: "The 'C' was symbolic of an almost completed circle of people who are gathering together for the perpetuation of those concepts you all deem important. The design was representative of their lineage and the very roots of your energy. The power and the support you will need are within you, and this was but a symbolic vision. You will soon receive much aid from those with whom you share these ties, and you in turn will be of equal value to them. Do not question, the pathway is before you."

I wanted to ask if I had any say in the matter, but decided against it. Maybe I really didn't want to know.

Early September, 1976: Joanne called. "I found

The Star Rover," she beamed over the phone. "I called twenty-two antique book stores, and was about to call a twenty-third, when I talked to a friend who is a psychic. I told her the story and she told me where to find the book. As it turned out it was the twenty-third bookstore on my list anyway."

Joanne took a couple of days to read it herself, then air-mailed it to us. Trenna and I had planned to spend the next weekend in a cabin hideaway on Oak Creek in Sedona, and took the book along. Once started, I couldn't put it down. London narrated the story of Darrell Standing, a fictionalized account of the prison life and adventures of Ed Morrell. The book began with Standing in prison awaiting execution, but told nothing of why he was there. It described the hideous agony of "the jacket," a device to torture inmates in solitary confinement, and how Standing developed self-hypnosis and astral-projection as techniques to survive confinement periods within it that lasted on one occasion a full ten days. While out of his physical body he could travel anywhere in the world, and also found that he could go backward in time and relive his own past lives. Much of the book is a detailed account of these prior incarnations. Because of the beautiful way Jack London used words to describe reincarnation and the reason for living, I will include a few paragraphs from the final pages of the book, which was published in 1915:

Pascal somewhere says: "In viewing the march of human evolution, the philosophic mind should look upon humanity as one man, and not as a conglomeration of individuals."

I sit here in Murderer's Row in Folsom, the drowsy hum of flies in my ears as I ponder that thought of Pascal. It is true. Just as the human embryo, in its brief ten lunar months, with bewildering swiftness, in myriad forms and semblances a myriad times multiplied, rehearses the entire history of organic life from vegetable to man; just as the human boy, in his brief years of boyhood, rehearses the history of primitive man in acts of cruelty and savagery, from wantonness of inflicting pain on lesser creatures to tribal consciousness expressed by the desire to run in gangs; just so, I, Darrell Standing, have rehearsed and relived all that primitive man was, and did, and became until he became even you and I and the rest of our kind in a twentieth-century civilization.

Truly do we carry in us, each human of us alive on the planet today, the incorruptible history of life from life's beginning. This history is written in our tissues and our bones, in our functions and our organs, in our brain cells, and in our spirits, and in all sorts of physical and psychic atavistic urgencies and compulsions.

What Pascal glimpsed with the vision of a seer, I have lived. I have seen myself that one man contemplated by Pascal's philosophic eye. Oh, I have a tale most true, most wonderful, most real to me, although I doubt that I have wit to tell it, and that you, my reader, have wit to perceive it when told. I say that I have seen myself that one man hinted at by Pascal. I have lain in the long trances of the jacket and glimpsed myself a thousand living men living the thousand lives that are themselves the history of the human man climbing upward through the ages.

Ah, what royal memories are mine as I flutter through the aeons of the long ago. In single jacket trances I have lived the many lives involved in the thousand-year-long odysseys of the early drifts of men. Heavens, before I was of the flaxen-haired AEsir, who dwelt in Asgard, and before I was of the red-haired Vanir, who dwelt in Vanaheim, long before those times I have memories (living memories) of earlier drifts, when, like thistle-down before the breeze, we drifted south before the face of the descending polar ice cap.

I have died of frost and famine, fight and flood. I have picked berries on the bleak backbone of the world, and I have dug roots to eat from fat-soiled fens and meadows. I have scratched the reindeer's semblance and the semblance of the hairy mammoth on ivory tusks gotten of the chase and on the rock walls of cave shelters when the winter storms moaned outside. I have cracked marrow bones on the sites of kingly cities that had perished centuries before my time or that were destined to be built centuries after my passing. And I have left the bones of my transient carcasses in pond bottoms, and glacial gravels, and asphalt lakes.

I have lived through the ages known today among the scientists as the Paleolithic, the Neolithic, and the Bronze. I remember when with our domesticated wolves we herded our reindeer to pasture on the north shores of the Mediterranean where now are France and Italy and Spain. This was before the ice sheet melted backward toward the pole. Many processions of the equinoxes have I lived through and died in, my reader, . . . only that I remember and that you do not.

I have been a Son of the Plough, a Son of the Fish, a Son of the Tree. All religions from the beginnings of man's religious time abide in me. And when the Dominie, in the chapel, here in Folsom of a Sunday, worships God in his own good modern way, I know that in him, the Dominie, still abide the worships of the Plough, the Fish, the Tree-ay, and also all worships of Astarte and the Night.

Sometimes I think that the story of man is the story of the love of woman. This memory of all my past that I write now is the memory of my love of woman. Ever, in the ten thousand lives and guises, I loved her. I love her now. My sleep is fraught with her, my waking fancies, no matter whence they start, lead me always to her. There is no escaping her, that eternal, splendid, ever-resplendent figure of woman.

Oh make no mistake. I am no callow, ardent

youth. I am an elderly man, broken in health and body, and soon to die. I am a scientist and a philosopher. I, as all the generation of philosophers before me, know woman for what she is—her weaknesses and meannesses and immodesties and ignobilities, her earth-bound feet and her eyes that have never seen the stars. But—and the everlasting irrefrangible fact remains: Her feet are beautiful, her eyes are beautiful, her arms and breasts are paradise, her charm is potent beyond all charm that has ever dazzled man; and, as the pole willy nilly draws the needle, just so, willy nilly, does she draw man.

Woman has made me laugh at death and distance, scorn fatigue and sleep. I have slain men, many men, for love of woman, or in warm blood have baptized our nuptials or washed away the stain of her favor to another. I have gone down to death and dishonor, my betrayal of my comrades and of the stars black upon me, for woman's sake—for my sake, rather, I desired her so. And I have lain in the barley, sick with yearning for her, just to see her pass and glut my eyes with the swaying wonder of her and of her hair, black with the night, or brown or flaxen, or all golden-dusty with the sun.

For woman is beautiful . . . to man. She is sweet to his tongue, and fragrance in his nostrils. She is fire in his blood, and a thunder of trumpets; her voice is beyond all music in his ears; and she can shake his soul that else stands steadfast in the drafty presence of the Titans of the light and of the Dark. And beyond his stargazing, in his far imagined heavens, Valkyrie or houri, man has fain made place for her, for he could see no heaven without her. And the sword in battle, singing, sings not so sweet a song as the woman sings to man merely by her laugh in the moonlight, or her love-sob in the dark, or by her swaying on her way under the sun while he lies dizzy with longing in the grass.

I sit in my cell now, while the flies hum in the drowsy summer afternoon, and I know that my time is short. Soon will they apparel me in the shirt without a collar. . . . But hush, my heart. The spirit is immortal. After the dark I shall live again, and there will be women. The future holds the women for me in the lives I am yet to live. And though the stars drift, and the heavens lie, ever remains woman resplendent, eternal, the one woman as, I, under all my masquerades and misadventures, am the one man, her mate.

When the book was finished, I walked with Trenna down to the creek, and we sat on the rocks in the middle of the swift current, discussing it. "I wish I knew more of the background," I told her. "It's a fictionalized account and there is no way to know how much of the story is fact. There are many, very heavy cross ties to my own affinities in those past lives and some strong childhood feelings too, I might add. Did Morrell actually relate his out-of-body past life experiences to London, or did London make them up, or even use his own?"

The next step in unraveling the mystery was library research. We found that nine years after the publication of Jack London's book, Ed Morrell wrote the true story of his experiences in his own volume titled *The 25th Man*. Naturally, the search was now in earnest, but we could not find the book. It wasn't listed in any of the 1924 book releases or *Books in Print* catalogues. An old man who runs an antique book store and makes his living finding out-of-print books told me, "I think it was self-published, so there is no knowing how many copies were actually printed. It is probably impossible to find."

This was another dead end, but another clue. Morrell was involved in metaphysics, hypnosis and self-publishing. If there were ever any interests or endeavors that had come easy to me in my life, it was these. In 1965 I'd started my own publishing company on a shoestring, publishing expensive books for the professional art and advertising market. Although the company was sold a few years ago, it is still the country's primary publisher of a very specialized style of turn-of-the-century engravings and illustrations volumes.

The Los Angeles Public Library listed *The 25th Man* in their files, but were unable to locate the book. It was now October and time to go on a month-long, multicity seminar tour of the northwestern portion of the country. I forgot about the case for the time being.

We arrived home in early November and among a table full of mail which was awaiting us was a box from Joanne. Inside, carefully packed in several inches of foam, was a perfect copy of *The 25th Man*, accompanied by a short note: "Herein find one early Christmas present. We located it through a book hunter in New York. Much love to both of you, Joanne."

Before the suitcases were unpacked I'd curled up by the fireplace and began to read.

THE
TWENTY-FIFTH
MAN

by Ed Morrell

Lone Survivor of the
California Feud Outlaws

The book is dedicated to "The Submerged Tenth of the World with Deepest Sympathy and Understanding." The foreword is written by George W. P. Hunt, Governor of Arizona—July 12, 1923. He talks of Morrell's victory over a barbarous prison system.

(NOTE: Although the story takes place in California, it was through Ed Morrell's work in Arizona that prison reforms were accomplished and the present Arizona penal system was established.)

In the Author's Preface Morrell describes how in 1912 he related his dungeon experiences to Jack London, "particularly those vivid wanderings in 'the little death' while undergoing torture in the jacket in the dungeon of San Quentin." He relates how the country's critics denounced *The Star Rover* upon its publication—"in the strongest language."

Morrell then explains: "I desire to state emphatically that the experiences of mind projection (astral-projection) in 'the little death' were very real to me, because I not only projected my mind through the power of self-hypnosis out of the dungeon and into the big living, moving world of today, influencing the lives of some who were destined to play a great part in my future life, but also I explored time through the ages reliving lives that I had lived just as surely as I live the present life. More, I was privileged in the dungeon to understand many strange complexities of my checkered career and the purpose for which I had been marked for suffering."

The book itself is a true western adventure, and prison horror story. Morrell was the youngest and twenty-fifth member of a band of settlers who turned outlaws over a land dispute with the railroad. It all takes place in the San Joaquin Valley and the Sierra Nevada Mountains, and is recorded as part of the history of California.

After his capture, Morrell was sentenced to life imprisonment in Folsom, and because of an escape attempt was later transferred to San Quentin. He was subjected to years of merciless cruelty and the tortures of a medieval prison system. Through self-hypnosis and astral-projection he survived to be released as the result of a documented series of psychic occurrences.

There were many affinity ties between the information in the book and my present life. As long as I can remember I've had dreams of hiding in the mountains with another man. I'm holding an old Winchester rifle and we're watching men coming towards us—far below. The exact situation Morrell found himself in on many occasions.

For years I've kept an old 1894 saddle-ring Winchester above the fireplace. I've worked on it and had gunsmiths work on it. Just holding the rifle has always given me a sense of peace and security I could never understand. It is the same model that Ed Morrell used.

"Why don't you hypnotise me?" Trenna asked. "If the knowledge is in your subconscious, you can establish a chakra link and maybe I can pick up something on the Morrell lifetime. I agreed and induced the trance, instructing her without direction to go back to the lifetime, if it was valid. She was soon relating a series of events that transpired after Ed's release, especially a situation in which he and his wife were paying a man to allow them to go through restricted files in an attempt to find evidence on corrupt prison practices. Some of this information, received in regression, has now been found to be correct.

Jean Perry, a regressive hypnotist from the Bio-Feedback Clinic in Des Moines, Iowa, was in Scottsdale in November, and volunteered to use a new nonverbal Oriental hypnosis technique to regress me. I accepted and asked her to take me to the Ed Morrell lifetime, if she could. Trenna and writer Alan Weisman were present and wrote questions on slips of paper which they handed to Jean, who asked them. I answered the questions and relived an hour and a half of portions of Morrell's life. Many of the situations were right out of his book, but most were new, and I provided exacting information, some of which has since been verified, but much of the data we are still attempting to find.

As of this writing I am eighty-five percent sure that I was Ed Morrell in my last earth incarnation—thinking in terms of sequential time. From the constant "now" perspective, we are parallel-selves, existing within different frequencies, yet influencing each other, for we are one and the same.

CHAPTER 18

EILEEN AND PAT
AND THE "LIGHT PEOPLE"

August, 1976: We were conducting a five-day seminar in the Scottsdale Sheraton Inn. It was the third day and all the participants were now well-conditioned hypnosis subjects. The program for the afternoon was a workshop and "group scan regression." This is a process of taking everyone quickly through six past lives—the last four lifetimes prior to the present life, then to the first life on earth, followed by their lifetime of highest evolvement. They are asked, while in regression, to rate each lifetime on a karmic scale of one to ten, positive, or negative as to how it is affecting their present incarnation. Then later in Higher-Self regression they can ask about any prior life which is exerting an excessive effect. The scan does not allow time for an in-depth examination of any of these lives, but enables the group to find dates, countries, occupations, and to relive a few important situations.

This regression had been conducted publicly many times and was well tested. But on this particular occasion, when I came to the instructions regarding the first lifetime on earth, I injected a new possibility. "I now want you to go backward in time, as we think of sequential time, to the very first lifetime you ever lived on the earth plane of existence. When I complete the instructions, you will see yourself in an important situation which transpired in this life. *If you are related to another planetary system, you may see yourself at the time of your arrival on earth."*

I'd never inserted such instructions before, and I haven't since, but I feel now that I was guided to do so in this case. Usually, upon awakening the group, I can count upon some general percentages. About half will see themselves in primitive existences and don't know what I'm talking about when I ask for the name of their country. A few will be partially in the nonphysical and partially in the manifest world— seemingly able to go back and forth and requiring no sustenance to live. The rest will usually see themselves in Atlantis, Lemuria, and occasionally later cultures.

During the first-life-on-earth portion of the scan, when I mentioned other planets, one woman in the middle of the group began to cry. Trenna immediately moved to her side and used special techniques to calm her down. The moment the group was awakened I left the podium to check on the woman who was upset. She was still crying and still in a trance. Anyone going deep enough to have such a reaction is capable of having the memories removed, so I now used a portable speaker to command her to leave the situation she was in and go to the happiest time she had ever experienced in her present life. She was soon smiling and relating the details of the situation as I asked her about it. The following instructions were then given: "All right, you are now going to find yourself in another environment . . . you are standing in a beautiful meadow . . . it is calm and peaceful here . . . and there are many leaves on the ground. Look down. Do you see the leaves? . . . O.k. I now want you to realize that the leaves are all the memories that you experienced while in regression, and a breeze is coming up . . . Can you feel the breeze? All right . . . the breeze is blowing away the memories . . . Look around you now . . . See the leaves blowing away . . . they are just blowing away . . . and soon they will be gone. . . . The leaves and memories are all gone . . . and in a moment I will awaken you and you'll feel good all over, happy and glad to be alive, but you will remember nothing that transpired while in regression."

I now motioned everyone else in the group back to their places and was walking away from my subject, whose name was Eileen, as I awakened her. She sat up and seemed quite content. Next I questioned the group about what they had received. Several individuals came to the speaker's platform and related their experiences. The overall percentages were generally the standard we'd come to expect. Then I directed myself to Eileen as if it were just a random question. "Eileen, what did you receive?"

"Oh, I'm afraid I fell asleep because I don't recall getting any impressions."

During our two-and-a-half-hour dinner break, before going back to the ballroom to perform individual directed regressions for the evening session, Trenna and I sat over a room-service dinner in our room. "There is really something we should find out about Eileen," she told me. "I picked up strange impressions and feelings that I can't even put into words while calming her down before you removed the memories."

"I don't know," I replied. "It might be something way too touchy to work with in a large group. I don't want to scare the hell out of our participants. As you know, in individual regression it can get pretty spooky. What do you know about her?"

"I talked to her after the session for quite some time," she said, flipping through our participants' questionnaire file book. "Here's her sheet."

I scanned the questionnaire sheet we ask all participants to fill out. Her name was Eileen Kaufman and she lives in the San Francisco bay area. Her husband is Bob Kaufman, a well-known contemporary poet. In the space asking for the participant's age there was a question mark. The rest of the sheet was only sparsely filled out, indicating she was involved in meditation, but no other metaphysical activities.

"What nationality do you think she is?" Trenna asked.

"I don't know. I can see three, maybe four pos-

192

sibilities. I guess she looks like a combination of them all. Possibly Oriental or Asian, combined with a darker-skinned race. She is certainly pretty, but I don't think I could guess her age either."

"From what she told me she has no idea of her origin, or age. All she knows is that she was born in the winter. She doesn't even know what country she was born in. The people who raised her were not related in any way and they were unable to provide her any information about her heritage. She's traveled all over the world trying to find a place, or a race, she felt an affinity for, but has yet to establish even the slightest mental ties. That's why she's here. She hoped through regression to find some leads.

"While I was calming her down I got flashes of bright lights and a silver tube, plus tremendous intensity. Why don't you regress her in front of the group tonight. I'll psychic monitor and if I see something heavy coming I'll clue you in advance. You can act in a split second to remove her from the environment if you need to."

I agreed, but felt anxiety about the situation. We talked to Eileen, explained everything that had transpired in the afternoon session, and offered to regress her individually if she felt up to it. She was more than anxious to have the chance to find out, through directly proposed questions, what the situation was all about.

That evening in the hypnosis lounger in front of the speaker's platform I began to individually hypnotise her. Trenna sat in a chair directly behind her and self-induced her own light trance. Intensive protection was invoked and I took excessive care to keep her calm and relaxed.

EILEEN
Regression Session

The following instructions were given: "You had a very intense reaction in this afternoon's session and although the memories have been blocked, your subconscious mind is still fully aware of what transpired and what this is all about. I now want you to allow information to come into your mind that will help to explain what upset you." (Instructions given.)

Q. Speak up now and tell me what you are receiving.
A. I see a swirl . . . swirling forms . . . light . . . blue . . . *it's me* . . . planet . . .
Q. Tell me more about this.
A. They won't let me talk.
Q. Who won't let you talk?
A. My superiors.
Q. Are you speaking of someone unseen who is here in the room with us now?
A. Yes . . . my monitor.
Q. Why won't they allow you to talk? This is a way for us to find information that could help you.
A. Seedling . . . seedling . . . a seedling does not speak. I can't talk . . . seedling.
Q. I'm not pressing them, but we are seeking understanding for your own sake. What will they allow you to communicate?
A. My vibrations are out of tune.
Q. What exactly happened this afternoon?
A. They took my breath. No breathing.
Q. Can you explain that a little more?
A. I can't.
Q. Why did they want you to experience this?
A. I'm not of this planet . . . I'm on this planet . . .

At this point Eileen began to become upset once again and her body began to tremble. She was immediately removed from hypnosis. Privately I might have forced her through the experience, but not in front of a ballroom full of people.

Trenna now volunteered. "Let me go under for her. You can do a chakra link and I know I can handle it."

"Trenna, the chakra link works both ways. She

194

could pick up directly from you even though she's wide awake," I replied, not liking the idea at all. "Besides, honey, you don't know what you're going to run into on this. Just think back on some of the real 'spookers' we've had."

"I really want to do it, Richard. I think it is important for some reason. Maybe for our own understanding. Obviously, for Eileen's sake. She's spent her entire life searching for answers about her past and this certainly is related to her past in some way or another."

Once more I agreed, on the condition that I use extensive spiritual protection, and that Trenna was willing to look at it as an observer instead of the technique in which she literally becomes the person in the past.

We now asked Eileen to sit between two of the seminar participants to whom she felt close. They would be touching her and feeding her energy. She was to stay totally conscious throughout the regression. Bruce Vaughan of Dallas, Texas, had already helped me work with a couple of cases of extreme depression and he now sat holding Eileen's hand.

Trenna took her place in the chair and I began the induction, then called upon her Guides and Masters to help and I asked for my own to be with her. Extensive spiritual protection was incorporated. Once she was in a deep trance I moved Trenna up into the Higher-Self mental levels and instructed her to create a viewing screen in her own mind. The screen was to have knobs which she could turn on to view prior life events. Now a chakra link was established between her and Eileen and she was instructed to go back into Eileen's past . . . to the situation we were attempting to find information about. "All right, Trenna, turn on the screen."

TRENNA
Regression for Eileen

Q. What are you perceiving at this time?

A. Standing in this . . . ah, it's a room, but it's not. Energy points . . . the essence which is Eileen is here . . . she's being judged. Swirling energy forms . . . they are life forms.

Q. What can you tell me about them?

A. There is no need for them to manifest into the physical, for them to do so would be to accept a lower life form. The reason Eileen felt as though she were losing her breath is that she was feeling what it was like to be in this nonphysical form. Although this is a much more highly evolved state, it is foreign to her and was thus frightening. She was shifting levels when she felt this.

Q. Was she going back to a previous time?

A. Yes . . . You see, Eileen was judged. She was a part of this higher life form on this planet and I can't see . . . I can't see from this perspective what she did wrong. She is in the building . . . it's not a physical room. It's hard to explain . . . it's all white and there are a lot of black voids on the outer edges of it. They really aren't talking but there is some form of communication transpiring . . . she is explaining her case. The entities that are involved in this come through these black voids to substantiate, or to disagree, with what she is saying. It's like a council . . . but they are all just swirling light or energy . . .

Q. What else can you tell me about the situation or beings themselves?

A. Eileen was banished. Eileen was part of the planet, or reality . . . and their punishment is to send beings down to a place like the earth . . . manifested into the physical . . . this is their punishment . . . there is nothing we can do! They're taking her in a silver . . . they're going to break her down somehow and then manifest her into a physical . . . They're taking me away!

She screamed loudly . . . then emitted a blood-curdling scream that could be heard all over the hotel.

The moment she said, "taking me," I knew she'd jumped my instructions and had become Eileen and was totally reliving the situation. I placed both hands on her for an instant energy transference and began an immediate removal. Out of the corner of my eye I could see that Eileen was hysterical. Most of the crowd had jumped to their feet and was on the verge of panic. One woman came racing forward holding an uplifted crucifix and was shouting for the evil spirits to leave in the name of Christ. The room was in chaos and all I could do for the moment was to get Trenna out of the situation. Bruce was doing a beautiful job of calming down Eileen and several people in the group were feeding her energy with their hands.

Trenna was now back in the Higher-Self, but still in a deep trance. The woman with the cross was continuing to carry on and Trenna yelled at her from the hypnotic state, "No . . . No! How can you stand in judgment of something you don't understand? . . . You can't relate to this. It is not evil . . . there is no evil here." The woman stopped and Trenna continued, "It is good that Eileen understands this. In so doing she can stop searching because she will never find any earthly ties. She is not of this earth, but she has so much to offer us through her own abilities to help people become in tune with themselves."

I wasn't about to let her go back into the "light people" environment again, but from the Higher-Self she continued to explain: "Eileen must not look at this as a negative thing, or to judge as they judged

197

her. They manifested her as a physical being. This afternoon she was transcending levels . . . one portion of her desires to return to nonphysical form. Yet she has found beauty in her physical form on this earth. She can help many of us here. Many of us are seedlings. She can rise above the punishment that was placed on her. Eileen is a very beautiful entity, and she should not be frightened of these beings. They were restraining some of the knowledge because it would be too much for her to accept at one time. She must forgive them, and this must be learned from this physical lifetime."

Q. Is there anything more you can communicate to us?

A. It was very frightening for Eileen to give up her nonphysical form for a physical one, but it was necessary for her to learn what she needed to learn. Through being here she is learning and she is also here to help others. There are many of us that have been implanted from other planets. We are a meshing . . . a combination of many evolutions.

Q. Is there anything more you can communicate to Eileen?

A. Reassure her that she is here for a purpose and we would all deeply appreciate her help. She must not search . . . she must forgive . . . not judge. These beings do not mean her harm. If she can use her earth time in the proper ways, she may return to her own world after completing her work here.

This was the end of the portion of the session, but from the Higher-Self Trenna told Eileen many personal things about her present life and advised her on future directions. Eileen later verified that all Trenna had told her was true and directly related to her present circumstances.

For two days following this experience Trenna was slightly dizzy and felt shaky. One of her arms also gave her trouble, but by the time the seminar was over she was fine. "I think I just got too close to an alien vibration," she explained. "It wasn't a matter of its being higher or lower, better or worse . . . just alien to our own sense of being."

This was the second time in a month I'd run into these "light people." A few weeks before, Pat Christensen, a twenty-nine-year-old housewife from Vancouver, Washington, also had a very unusual experience. In a room of about twenty people I'd hypnotised her and directed her to return to an important previous incarnation.

PAT
Regression Session

Q. Tell me what you are experiencing?

A. I see a light wall . . . it's not material . . . it's a wall of light. I'm standing at its base. The wall is a circular . . . It feels like I'm getting myself from this light. I'm standing inside what seems like a domed building in a wall of light for the purpose of receiving energy. There is a corridor that extends from the light . . . I'm now in this corridor . . . it's taking me outside . . . I don't want to go. (Pat later explained that she was light, or an energy force as opposed to a physical being.)

Q. All right, let's let go of this and move forward in time just a little ways. (Instructions given.)

A. I'm being tested . . . she keeps asking me questions . . . I don't want to be here, I don't want to be here . . . (She is now starting to cry and is almost screaming, so I immediately removed her from the environment and moved her into the Higher-Self in an attempt to understand what was happening.)

199

Q. Can you speak up now and explain to me what was happening a few moments ago . . . why you were so upset?

A. Pat was experiencing . . . (A channel had broken through. I can spot the vocal patterns in two seconds. This is a matter of another entity, a discarnate, or another aspect of the subject's own personality using the vocal cords to communicate. The moment it happens I become totally dominant, and have often been asked later by my observers why I suddenly "got mad" at my subject. It is not a matter of getting mad, but it is a matter of being so firm that it often appears that way. The main reason for this is that things can get out of hand very quickly and you never allow the alien identity to gain any control if it looks as if it might be misused. Over the years, on various occasions, I've been snarled at and hissed at and told by these spooks that I had no control over them. This is never true, for they are easily controlled if you know exactly what you are doing, but it does scare the observers. A room full of bug-eyed people with their hair standing on end doesn't make the situation any easier. In Pat's case the voice was a total change from her own, yet soft and gentle and sounded quite old. I decided to allow it to continue as long as there was no evidence of manipulation.) Pat was experiencing the energies that are within her which she refuses to release. She knows this . . . she has been consciously aware of it, but she refuses to accept her abilities. She shall be forced to continue on until she is willing to accept the fact that she has this wisdom. She has available to her all abilities and there is nothing she cannot do."

Q. Who am I talking to?

A. You are talking to the wisdom of this soul. I have no name . . . I am a source . . . I am a part of all that is. Pat has to learn to become truly aware of two things. She had written to herself the essence of all desire and belief, and she knows it. As soon as she accepts it then everything will fall into place. Pat is full of love and when she can express her love as she knows it in her heart there will be no stopping her. That is why she is here with you, Dick. She knows, but has refused to accept, and she is in search of someone to hold her hand instead of standing up for herself when she knows she can.

Q. I want you to tell me about what Pat was experiencing earlier.

A. She was experiencing something that relates to this lifetime. She is a student of the earth, but she is not as you think a member of the earth. She has not been incarnated many times as you are in search of in regressing her. Instead she comes from far corners of the cosmos and she is here on her second trip only. You see she is quite like an alien in your sense of the word.

Q. Could you tell me about her first earth life?

A. This was in the land where there is much, much sand. I cannot answer all your questions even though you think I should.

Q. Is there anything else you would like to communicate?

A. No. (Very softly.)

Q. All right, I now want Pat to come back in. (Instructions given.) Pat, I now want to ask you some questions.

A. I really don't want to do this . . . I really don't want to do this. (She is now very upset again, so I removed all of the memories of what had transpired and awakened her feeling relaxed as if she had taken a nice nap.)

(End of regression session.)

I gave a copy of the recording of the session to Pat's husband and told him to explain it all to her later. Then when he felt it was right and she could be objective about the experience, he should play her the tape. We'd all talk about it after that.

This regression took place in Scottsdale, but several months later we were in Portland for a seminar and I had a chance to have breakfast with Pat. She was now attending a hypnosis school to learn to be a hypnotist. "I've just got to find out more about all of this," she explained. She also told me that a local hypnotist performed many regressions, and on numerous occasions had encountered the "light people."

What does it all amount to? I don't know. In nearly a year of national seminar touring I've worked with thousands of people all over the country. After the completion of each group scan regression, I now ask, "Did anyone, by any chance, perceive themselves, in one of the six lifetimes, as a light form, or energy being? Maybe you saw yourself as a shimmering, or pulsating light . . . probably white, yellow white, or light blue in color?"

Without fail I've found in every city that six to seven percent of the hands go up. They all share a wide-eyed expression of expectation. Usually they perceived themselves as a light being during the first-life-on-earth portion of the session. None of these participants had received any prior programming from me, for nothing of the previous encounters was ever mentioned.

Maybe the earth is simply a school, or learning place, for misguided light people, or energy beings. Maybe all of my subjects had similar hallucinations. In Chapter 10 I related Kingdon Brown's trance words to the effect that we are working towards a transcendence to become nonphysical light people. If true, this might be what we were before and we desire to go home. It could relate to genetic manipulation, or seeding of the earth by extraterrestrials. I have enough information on outer space involvement with the earth to write two books, but there are enough writers already covering that subject.

For now, the light people remain untouchable, but at least we know about them. I for one will continue to seek additional knowledge and understanding about their relationship to our history and more important, their ability to influence or manipulate our present reality.

CHAPTER 19

THE FREQUENCY SWITCH—
ANOTHER CONCEPT
BEYOND REINCARNATION

March, 1977: We made the decision to move back to the Phoenix Valley. As much as I love the mountains, Scottsdale, Arizona, which had been our home for many years, remains my favorite place on earth. It is a resort town of about 75,000 people. The buildings are old western or Spanish and palm trees line the streets. Resorts and tourism is the primary industry and warm friendly people are the order of the day. A zealous city government restricts all building and commercialism such as signage. It is the only place in the country where you will find a giant Holiday Inn sporting a sign in white letters so small you can hardly read them from the street.

We found a home on the saguaro desert in the Mc-Dowell Mountain foothills northeast of the city. There is plenty of room for horse corrals, and for the dogs and kids to run free. The Pima Indian Reservation covers the miles between us and the city center, and at night the lights of the entire valley fill the family room picture window.

It was good to be back to stay. Our Prescott contacts would always be maintained, and we would occasionally return to camp out by those cool mountain creeks during the hot summer months. Psychic guidance directed us to that area to mentally regroup and to meet people who would prove to be invaluable to us. Now it was time to come home. Business availabilities and the close proximity of the Phoenix airport had become increasingly important to our work.

A Super-Seminar was planned in Scottsdale for July, 1977, and I'd promised to do several new regressive group explorations that were not yet fully developed. The seven-day affair would be attended mostly by those who had participated in previous sessions in other cities. Richard Bach, Brad Steiger, Kingdon Brown, David Paladin and many others would be guest speakers and help to guide the sessions.

In preparation for this event we began research gatherings at our home with people who volunteered to be guinea pigs. No one is ever in any danger, even of a fearful experience, if they don't want it, for I always include a self-releasing suggestion as part of every induction. But when you're hypnotising a hundred or two hundred people at a time, you want it to be effective for the highest possible percentage of participants.

For years the doomsdayers and soothsayers have been predicting holocausts and earth changes, yet every bit of psychic input I have personally received points to a "frequency switch" that will transpire around the year 2000; and individuals who are "ready" will transcend into an age of peace and altruism. Those who have not evolved to this level of understanding will experience the reality they themselves created with the power of their own minds. In other words, they can experience hellfire and brimstone in one reality, while simultaneously, for many, a world of peaceful coexistence will come into being and continue to exist as if nothing ever happened.

This would assume that in addition to the past and present, as we perceive them, other immediate realities might now, or could conceivably at some time, exist just a frequency away, in the same physical space.

What do I base this "frequency transition" concept upon? My own and Trenna's psychic input, David

Paladin's experiences and concepts, and contact with Kandinsky, who channels through David, plus far more fact-based case histories than I can begin to relate in this chapter.

Journeys Out of the Body by Robert Monroe is the most objective book available on astral projection. In it the author describes the out-of-body experience of finding himself on several occasions within a reality quite similar, yet totally alien, to our own. On each visit, he was drawn to a particular man and actually took possession of his body. As a probability, on these occasions he could have transcended frequencies through the altered mental state and was drawn to another exploration of his own potential which simultaneously exists in the here and now.

The American Indian Ghost Dance phenomenon has long been one of my favorite subjects of interest and study. In 1890 a Paiute messiah named Wavoka was supposedly resurrected and founded the Ghost Dance religion. He taught the dance to all Indians who came to him and showed them how to make special shirts painted with magic symbols for protection and power intensifications. According to Wavoka, by dancing this dance, they would transcend the negative reality of the white man, and by the following spring would find themselves in an environment of the past—with great herds of buffalo and no white men. The ritual spread throughout numerous tribes and became a religious fervor, panicking the white soldiers and resulting in Sitting Bull's death.

The Ghost Dance was considered an idealistic dream, born out of persecution and desperation, and once controlled it was dismissed. Yet it has always been my belief that the dance worked because so many thousands of Indians believed it with such intensity. They created their own reality by switching frequencies.

If other realities actually exist in the here and now, could hypnosis open the doors to allow us to perceive them visually, or mentally project into them? I had pondered the questions, and potential techniques of exploration, for the better part of a year. It was time to find out.

THE FREQUENCY SWITCH GROUP SESSION

Six individuals, all well conditioned hypnosis subjects I'd worked with before, were invited over to our house for an evening session. I explained my concept of the frequency switch possibility thoroughly, but carefully avoided any possibility of programming their expectations.

Hypnosis was induced, spiritual protection invoked, and the following instructions were then given. "Within the superconscious area of your mind there exists a complete understanding of the totality of life and existence. In your conscious, waking state you are limited to the boundaries of your present reality, but mentally you are without limitation. If other realities exist in the here and now, you have the ability to mentally project into them . . . to become an observer of these other worlds, or alternate frequencies of our present world. If exploration is possible, your own subconscious mind will choose the reality you desire to explore at this time." (Transition instructions given.)

"You are now there and I want you to look around you and perceive every detail of the environment you now find yourself within." The six subjects are now lying silently on the floor, all in deep hypnosis and all, hopefully, receiving some form of experience. Tonight I would be asking for no verbal answers, but would direct them into experiences, if possible, and then give them strong suggestions to remember what they encountered so they could talk about it when awakened.

Three minutes passed before I gave the next instructions. "Can you move within this reality? Are there other life forms there with you, and if so can you get close to them, can you become part of them? Perceive those things similar to your own conscious

207

reality, and those things that are alien to you." After each question I would remain silent for several minutes. Then they were given five minutes freedom to go exploring on their own. Additional questions were asked, and then an hour after the session began, I awakened the group with the positive suggestion to feel good and relaxed, and to remember every detail they had perceived.

It wasn't the normal awakening reaction after a group session. Their eyes were wider than usual, and they were shaking their heads and looking at me as if I'd just instructed them to go fly off the roof. One woman simply buried her head in her knees. "I need to know what happened." I smiled. "Before you forget any of it, take turns passing the microphone around the room."

Rachel, age 30, housewife: At first I was flowing through solid geometric shapes, like light through a window . . . a stained glass window, for there was intense color. Then it faded away and I was the light. A form . . . not like the form of a human being, but like a pulsating energy . . . white, or yellow-white, against a blue black void. There were other lights. At times many, and occasionally only a few. Your questions didn't seem to relate to anything, and I know I began to turn you off . . . and as I did I began to get into being the light form. I can't put it into words, but I know I was exploring concepts within myself and with others. Someone would send out data, like the entire *Encyclopedia Britannica,* and it would be mentally digested within a split second, then discussed, argued within a couple more seconds . . . then on to another concept. Everything was mind. . . . Everything flowed into and through everything else. I just don't know how to describe it any better. (Rachel was totally unaware of our light people encounters I discussed in the earlier chapter.)

Jeffrey, age 37, doctor: Every time I get around you, Richard, I end up with my mind being blown. Often it has changed my life for the better. Tonight . . . I'm not really sure I needed tonight (laughter

among group). At first I thought I was right here
. . . that maybe I'd transferred to somewhere like
northern California. There were pine trees, mountains . . . a normal woodsy environment. I was
standing in a clearing and all of a sudden I saw a
horse-drawn wagon going by in the distance . . .
through the trees. I ran over to the edge of the trees
to get a better look and it was the damndest-looking
wagon I've ever seen. It had one wheel in the front,
two in the back, and was brightly colored . . . red with
flower designs all over it. A man and a woman, at least
I think it was a man and a woman, they both had
bowl-cut hairdos, were in the wagon. They wore very
strange clothes, but appeared to be human. She was
driving the wagon. Soon other wagons came by, and
finally I stepped out on the road and waved . . . but
nobody saw me. They looked right through me. The
road was paved . . . perfectly smooth, and pure white.
There were road signs that showed symbols, but I
don't know what they meant. The signs seemed to be
made of a plasticlike material.

One of your instructions must have triggered a
location change, because all of a sudden the road
disappeared and I was flying, or more accurately tum-
bling, through the air. Then I stabilized and was
flying over a city. It was all white, glimmering white
and as contemporary-looking as anything we would
know today. There were elevated walkways everywhere, and trees and flowers within the city. I could
not see any visible form of transportation. It was all
so contemporary that I felt the horse-drawn carts must
have simply been for diversionary purposes, like we'd
rent horses in Central Park. I don't know any more,
and I certainly don't know what to think of it.

Wanda, age 27, fine artist: After listening to Rachel
and Jeffrey's stories I think I was short-changed. I
felt as if I was water. It was one of the weirdest experiences I've ever had, for I was part of it and all of
it at once. The physical sensation was a drop of water
flowing down a creek . . . over rocks, splashing and

209

twisting and turning . . . dropping down small water-falls and flowing on. That's it, folks.

Lori, age 33, executive secretary: I'm afraid I don't have anything to tell you. I really feel that I experienced something . . . maybe something very heavy, but it was gone when you woke us up. I sit here now, like I've often done in the morning, trying to remember a dream, but am unable to do it.

George, age 42, retail shop owner: I don't know if Jeff was sending to me, or if I was sending to him, or if maybe we both went to the same alternate reality? I too saw a city such as the one he described, only from ground level. I didn't see any horse-drawn carts. Anyway, I was right there in the middle of the activities and the people and it was soon apparent that no one could see me. It was like being invisible and walking through a crowded downtown street . . . right through people. The people themselves were all quite pretty, although they were all ages. All were dressed in variations of light-colored togas and wore their hair in similar, simple fashion. I could tell the women by their breasts and hairless legs. I didn't see any form of motorized transportation either, but there was no place where it could have been used. As I walked through the streets I had the feeling that it was a community of about a hundred thousand people, nestled in a wooded, mountain environment. There was a large circular tower in the center of the city, it looked like a Flash Gordon version of a lighthouse, but I don't know what it was for.

When you asked us to notice similar and alien things, I noticed that I'd never seen flowers like the ones that were growing there. They were totally different . . . all of them. Yet most of the trees were like our trees. I could hear the people talking and there is no way to relate it. Just like a foreign language, and meaningless to me. I did stop and watch an artist working in what appeared to be a park. He didn't use a brush, or anything we are familiar with. His paint was in sheets like a thick sheet of paper and he would break off pieces and apply them, edge first, with

210

finger pressure. They seemed to melt into his board, or canvas, or whatever it was. He was painting a young lady lying in the grass and they were obviously very much in love.

Anne, age 25, housewife and substitute grade school teacher: Well, maybe I didn't follow your instructions as well as I should have, Dick. Maybe I just left my body and messed around on the astral plane, because wherever I was, thought form was the reality. If I thought bright yellow light, there it was. I conjured up some horrible-looking devils and when they began to scare me I created angels to chase them away. This went on faster and faster, until the images were almost on top of each other, they were coming in and going out so fast. I found myself thinking, what is real? What has value? What remains? The next thing I knew there was someone else there before me and they reached out and touched my cheek and I could feel a warmth that flowed through my entire body. It was more than a warmth, it was a glow. So I reached out and touched their cheek and the glow seemed to intensify. I couldn't tell you now what the other person even looked like and I think the experience was symbolic . . . maybe the essence of love. I don't mean that to sound corny, because the experience certainly wasn't corny. You then asked if we could become part of another life form and I stepped forward and we were one, and a twirling began and as it did I began to pull everything to me . . . like a whirlpool, sucking everything in the world to me and they were me. It was really a trip . . . especially for me. I'm not into this love thy neighbor evolution of the soul bit. I'm a housewife who takes good care of her kids, keeps a balanced checkbook, and thinks flower children and hippies are weirdos we'd be better off without.

Several sessions, with different people, followed, and the results were as diversified as those of the initial session. A city similar to the one mentioned by

211

Jeff and George was mentioned two more times. It could be a city beyond our normal abilities of perception, that sits right where my home sits now. The Scottsdale of a different reality. They could have gone back to Atlantis, or forward into the future. There is simply no way to know for sure. In the forthcoming seminar in Scottsdale I will use the same instructions to guide two hundred people at the same time into an alternate reality. New patterns may emerge, and new directions to research.

CHAPTER 20

SUPPORTIVE MATERIAL
FROM THE DOCTORS

The first nine years of my involvement with the psychic/metaphysical world were much the same from a career perspective. An author, artist, psychic researcher—the work was interesting and always different, and Arizona people were supportive. Then, with the publication of *You Were Born Again to Be Together,* our simple uncomplicated world turned upside down.

In May of 1976, Trenna and I appeared on Tom Snyder's NBC Tomorrow Show, and I conducted the first nationally televised past life hypnotic regression. The David Susskind Show and hundreds of other local and national T.V. and radio appearances followed. Everything we did led to something else.

A momentum was obviously building. We appeared at new age festivals and the interest in our seminars doubled and tripled and then skyrocketed. Tonight I was standing backstage, waiting to go out and talk to an overflow crowd, and Trenna caught me smiling to myself.

"What's funny?" she asked.

"I was thinking about the night we opened The Hypnosis Center in Scottsdale," I replied.

"Oh." She smiled back. A knowing smile.

That night had been one of my bigger lessons in

humility. A nice brochure had been printed and mailed to several hundred people. Flyers were distributed, and a sizeable newspaper ad announced the "Free Grand Opening at 7:30 Wednesday Evening." At the appointed time only one man was there. I decided to wait awhile to begin my lecture, but half an hour later only my secretary and the patient man in the front row sat staring at me.

The Hypnosis Center originally had twenty-five chairs. The next day I went and bought twenty-five more and vowed such a thing would never happen again. It didn't.

June, 1977: With only minimal announcements, over 800 people had paid the sponsoring organization to attend tonight's commercial preview of the forthcoming past life seminar. Grant Gudmundson, a psychic, new age speaker and the seminar host would talk. Large screen video tapes of actual regressions would be shown, and then I would do a forty-five minute wrap-up lecture. In Houston, Texas, a few weeks before we'd had an audience of a thousand. (I insist that the actual seminars usually remain very small.)

"Look at the difference in the interest in reincarnation and metaphysics in just these few years," I mused, waiting for Grant's introduction. Trenna just smiled and shook her head.

"You're on, Richard . . . break a leg!" She gave me a kiss as I moved past her.

Alan Weisman wouldn't be here for this seminar. He was off in Mexico writing a book about a Catholic priest who raises orphan children. For months Alan had followed us around from seminar to seminar, writing a book about our work and activities and the results of participation. He'd ask a million questions, was often impossible to tolerate, but eventually we became used to it, or he mellowed out . . . I'm not sure which. Now I found myself missing his objective presence.

Alan is a feature stringer for the Phoenix *Republic* and a freelance writer/photographer for magazines all over the country. His book about us, titled *We Immortals**, was now in print and I had to admit it was an excellent job of investigative reporting. He used Trenna and me as the focus, but drew a larger journalist picture of the entire Aquarian Age—the new spiritual consciousness movement and all its cultural implications. All the personalities were there—the objective truth-seekers, the "spiritual groupies," the psychics, psychologists, hypnotherapists and even statements from the fundamentalist clergy who oppose me.

The psychologist's statements were of special interest to me. I've always shared our techniques with all professionals who were interested in incorporating them into their practice. Alan had followed up on several such cases.

Dr. Edith Fiore, Ph.D., practices in the San Jose area of California. After attending a hypnosis workshop at the Esalen Institute, she began to incorporate hypnotherapy into her work. Her belief in the possibility of reincarnation came as the result of her patients' unexplainable reactions to her hypnotic instructions. When she directed them to go back to the original cause of their present emotional discomfort, many went back into what appeared to be previous lifetimes.

When asked about this by the reporter from a California newspaper, Dr. Fiore said, "There are just too many cases of people who have gone through regression and come up with valid information. I've had patients with obesity problems who were regressed to former lifetimes where they starved to death. As soon as they relived the experience, they started to lose weight. In the final analysis it doesn't really matter whether it's fantasy or reality. What's important is that the person gets well."

I met Edith and her husband, Greg LeMons, a San Francisco area filmmaker, at a very small seminar I conducted in Prescott. She'd read my book and wanted

---

* To be published by Pocket Books in 1978.

to learn more about the techniques I was using. As it worked out I'm sure I learned as much, if not more, from her, for she openly shared all information and some therapy methodologies which were totally new to me.

The following statements by Edith are from *We, Immortals:*

The more I do this kind of research, the more I'm convinced that we must look beyond the obvious for solutions to people's problems. One woman even traced her fear of her father back to the womb. Under hypnosis she gave a detailed account of a fight between her parents, remembered from long ago. But when we checked out the facts to determine exactly when it happened, it turned out she hadn't even been born yet—her mother was just three months pregnant with her. Somehow, she had been conscious even then.

Among professional societies for clinical hypnosis I would have to say that reincarnation therapy is neither widely accepted nor totally ignored. In my area, San Jose, I know of only one other therapist who is using it. And, I haven't gotten that much feedback myself yet, because it's only been in the past year that I've begun to believe in its effectiveness enough to use it extensively. One interesting thing, though: so far, I've had no real disapproval from the church, and several of my patients have asked their clergymen how they feel about reincarnation. One priest even replied that it is not antithetical to believe in it and still be a good Catholic.

Weisman also interviewed Dr. Arlene Koeppen, Ph.D., from Richardson, Texas. Arlene and her husband Larry, who is also a counselor and presently working on his doctoral dissertation on the use of computers in counseling, had attended one of our two-day seminars in Dallas, and a five-day seminar in Scottsdale. She describes her basic orientation as, "humanistic with a strong metaphysical influence."

In his book Alan writes:

For Arlene, an important moment came when Dick was able to elicit under hypnosis a response from a patient she knew to have undergone months of conventional therapy without much success. Dick's constant admonition to "trust your mind" has become her motto in her own approach to therapy. Although regression itself is not yet part of her therapy methods, "my own regressive experiences have had a significant impact on my work. What I now do in trying to understand why a person behaves in a certain manner is to 'become' that person. When I trust my mind, it works. Sometimes, it is a little tricky learning how to 'unbecome' after entering deep levels of empathy or understanding."

"Behind the message, 'trust your mind,'" [she told Alan] "is the perhaps subtler message to accept ourselves. We're living faster, 'future-shock' lives, being required to make decisions with less information, and this increases the stress and anxiety in our lives. More and more, we encounter technologies and institutions which are beyond our understanding and control. Our politicians and religious leaders are rapidly losing credibility through increased ineffectiveness in the face of increased complexity." [So what do we do?] "I see metaphysics as a set of constructs and beliefs from which I can reclaim responsibility and control for my own life. Dick attracts other people who accept the premise that there is more to this life than the observable, objective reality and affords them a demonstration of the philosophy along with an opportunity to explore reality on an inner dimension."

As part of a national tour you are always asked to

do newspaper interviews, and afterwards the reporters usually attempt to seek local supportive or adverse material to include as part of the story.

Bea Pixa of *The San Francisco Examiner* wrote just such an article about our work and contacted Freda Morris, Ph.D., a Bay Area hypnotherapist.

Freda, formerly assistant professor of psychology at UCLA's medical school, believes a good case can be made for reincarnation. One client, she says, suffered asthma from girlhood, which during a hypnotic trance, turned out to be the result of never having mourned a lover in a previous life. She was reliving it in her asthma attacks, but after just one session, by reliving the experience, she never had asthma again, claims Morris.

Morris herself recalls a lifetime as a newspaperman in Sacramento. Though she is willing to concede that it could all be fantasy, she is clearly on the side of the reincarnation believers.

Hopefully we'll soon see the day when more than a handful of medical professionals will consider regressive hypnosis techniques worthy of therapeutic consideration. It has only been a few years that the AMA has recognized hypnosis as a valid technique. The same is true of acupuncture, although they still don't know how or why it works.

CHAPTER **21**

WHO NEEDS AWARENESS?

Who needs awareness? Everyone, if they are mentally evolving in synchronization with the presently accelerating society/earth frequencies. It will be through self-awareness that we will survive and function in a superior way in the midst of ever-increasing intensity.

Most people in this country have satisfied their basic needs for: 1) food, 2) rest, 3) shelter, and 4) feelings of safety. These are basic on a "need hierarchy" list, and it is only when they are satisfied that we become aware of our higher needs. After security we need 5) to belong, to be accepted, and 6) to give and receive love. For many people this will be the extent of their need list, and once satisfied their quests will be for material advancement. For the sake of communication I'll call such people "materialists." They function well in the present sociological environment, but may find it increasingly difficult with the acceleration of change.

There is a "new-age" individual who is not satisfied with the aforementioned need list. Self-actualization must follow the satisfaction of the lower needs. For these people the new higher needs will become just as real as their first need of food.

219

Ego Needs
(Materialist and/or New Age)
7) The need to be independent.
8) The need to achieve status and recognition.

New Age Needs
9) The need to understand and control personal reality.
10) The need to fulfill one's own potential.
11) Enlightenment/Inner-harmony/Transcendence

Many people become involved with psychic and metaphysical concepts at the time of a crisis in their lives. They feel that they "found" this philosophy at exactly the right time. In reality, it is more likely that their pathway towards awareness is what actually caused the turbulence in their lives. Intuitively they already "had" the philosophy; they just had to rearrange their reality to encompass it.

"Why didn't I consciously realize it sooner?" is an often-asked question.

You were always moving in the proper direction, but you needed to work out old karmic situations on the way. The awareness was always there, beckoning like a lighthouse in the darkness—in intuitive understanding gleaned from all of your lifetimes. It was drawing you towards your subconscious goal of evolving into a fully aware, transcended, new age individual.

Evolution can be painful. These needs can cause conflicts in any area of your life . . . especially interpersonal relationships. It is one of the primary reasons for the high divorce rate. The couple started off on basically the same "need level." As they satisfied needs, one stopped climbing while the other continued. The materialist cannot understand or relate to the need level of the new-ager, or vice-versa. The result is often the re-pairing with new partners who can relate.

Evolution can be beautiful. You will learn that you are only limited by the boundaries of your beliefs, and through your expanded awareness you will begin to create your own reality of self-imposed success and happiness.

The awareness/consciousness movement which has taken the country by storm, I call *metaphysics,* and I recently found it necessary to redefine the term. The following statement is the result of Trenna and me spending many hours attempting to capture the very essence of our belief within the smallest number of words.

Metaphysics is a philosophy/religion/science of self in relationship to reality. It incorporates the concepts of reincarnation and karma into an evolutive principle of love, freedom, and self-responsibility. It is an awareness of psychic techniques and ancient methodologies, and the ability to use them, to create your own reality. It teaches that by mastering inner harmony, you achieve absolute control of your destiny. It will be the wisdom of a New-Age Race that will transcend fear to lead the way into the Aquarian Age.

CHAPTER **22**

FUTURE FREEDOM—
CREATING YOUR
OWN REALITY

As a summary of the basic concepts in this book:

1. There is evidence that we are multidimensional beings, with separate-selves existing in the past, present, and future.

2. These separate-selves are affecting us and we feel what is classically considered the karmic results. We may also be experiencing the effects of numerous unseen influences.

3. Important relationships in your life are related to ties in other historic periods, in other realities, or through similar present-day partnerships of your separate-selves.

4. Through inner harmony we rise above the manifestation of external effects whether they are self-created or are the results of the experiences of our separate-selves in the past, present or future.

5. Self-established inner harmony will result in expanding our own awareness, and will also have an evolutive effect on our separate-selves. If a forthcoming transcendence is a goal, all of our

separate-selves may need to evolve to an equal degree.

6. Inner harmony equals wisdom, which erases karma, resulting in *freedom*.

7. Regardless of your belief in reincarnation, karma, separate-selves, a constant now, or creation concepts, *as a medical fact*—the subconscious mind *can* be reprogrammed. What mind has created, mind can change. You can create your own reality of inner harmony. If the immediate goal is inner harmony, the obvious question is what is it, and how do I achieve it?

What is it? It is being at peace with yourself, or knowing self-satisfaction. You do not allow others to affect you negatively, knowing that they are doing what they have to do, and only what you think about what they are doing is affecting you . . . the concept of nonjudgment. It is also a matter of rising above fear through the realization that there is nothing to fear.

If you could accomplish this self-satisfaction, nonjudgment and elimination of fear, you would literally evolve beyond worldly negative effects.

How do I achieve it? In Chapter 9, Karma Without the "Hocus Pocus," I discussed the first step in detail. Begin to monitor your thoughts to eliminate all negative, fear thoughts from your mind. Now I will begin to discuss techniques that can be of great value in helping you to accomplish this. No matter what you might find out about your past, present-parallels, or future lifetimes through hypnotic techniques, you will still approach the future in the same way—by reprogramming the input into your subconscious mind. As I have already stated, the subconscious functions only according to programming. It operates like a cold machine, but it is more than willing to help if programmed properly. So you have to be the programmer, and to do this you need to know how the machine works and how to get the most out of it.

The first thing to remember is that the subconscious cannot tell the difference between fact and fantasy—

between real experiences and imagined experiences. So the next obvious step is to figure out the best methodology to fool the machine into creating the desired result.

There is certainly no equally effective way for everyone to program their computer, but there are many very effective techniques. These techniques have been used by happy, successful people throughout history. They are being used today under many names and with variations. Some books on witchcraft will give you the same methodologies you will find used in psycho-cybernetics. An esoteric volume on metaphysics would call the same techniques "pre-monstration," "positive affirmation," "aggressive meditation" or "cosmosis" . . . and there are many other names, but they all amount to basically the same thing *and they work*. They have been working for centuries.

My own technique is "self-hypnosis." I'm certainly not saying it is better than any of the others I've mentioned. One of them might be better for you, but I know and favor this technique, because I feel it facilitates reprogramming and accelerates change, especially when you combine the ancient methodologies with the modern technology of the cassette tape recorder. The consistency of a tape-recorded program intensifies the message to the subconscious.

There are many professionally produced programming tapes, but you can do it yourself.

Before proceeding you should have some understanding of hypnosis. It is probably the most misunderstood of all human potentials, and is usually thought of as a mystical "unknown" . . . some magical form of control. Most of us are very wary of what we don't understand, and especially of hypnosis. Movies, books and stage hypnotists have given the world a false image of an extremely valuable and natural tool.

Hypnosis is a setting aside of the conscious mind, a narrowing of the attention span to one thing. It is an altered state of consciousness and a state of hypersuggestibility. So, positive suggestions given while in a state of self-hypnosis or directed hypnosis are extremely effective in helping to create positive change, or in opening doors to memories locked in the subconscious mind.

You probably think of stage hypnosis when you think of hypnosis. This is by far the most dramatic visualization, and since control is seemingly involved, most people become personally wary of the entire concept. I want to point out that any fourth-rate hypnotist can find the one person in ten, in his audience, who will make a good stage subject. If the hypnotist has a good line of chatter, he can amuse the audience, but he is not controlling his subject. A directly proposed hypnotic suggestion could not make the person do anything against his morals, religion or self-preservation. If such a suggestion were given, the subject would either refuse to comply or would wake up. The hypnotist does have the subject completely relaxed and open to suggestion—a state of hypersuggestibility—and so relaxed that he doesn't care that the audience is watching. The hypnotist may tell him that there is a bird sitting on the head of everyone in the audience, and to go out and pick the bird he likes best and return to the stage. The subject does see the bird and follows the instructions. The hypnotist then tells him that he has one minute to teach the bird a trick, and the audience usually goes into hysterics as they watch him comply by working with the invisible bird. This is funny and harmless, and works because the subject is capable of a somnambulistic hypnotic trance level. Most people are not, but they are often hypnotised without knowing it, and this is not funny. It isn't that they are doing anything they can't remember during that time, it is simply that they don't realize how effectively they are being manipulated. The vast majority of people do not recognize the state of hypnosis. There are actually over twenty overlapping levels of hypnosis, but for the sake of simplification I will break them down into three:

1. *Light trance:* The subject becomes very relaxed, although he will probably not feel that he

225

is hypnotised. He remains fully aware of everything going on around him. If a car drives by, or someone walks across the room, he will be aware of it. The majority of people reach this level very easily.

2. *Medium trance:* The subject becomes totally relaxed and is completely open to suggestion. He can feel or relive any suggested event. He may be aware, to a degree, of what is going on around him, but it will not distract him.

3. *Deep-level trance:* Only one person in ten achieves a somnambulistic level. A subject in this level of hypnosis will not remember what he has experienced while in hypnosis unless specifically commanded to do so upon awakening.

In working at home with self-hypnosis you will be working in any of these levels. As you become hypnotically conditioned you will go deeper each time you go under, until you reach your "natural" level. For most, it will be in the medium area. Before proceeding, I would like to explain how hypnosis is used in public, for this will help you to fully understand it.

The two most famous lawyers in this country are highly trained hypnotists, as are many of Madison Avenue's most successful advertising executives, and a large number of the fundamentalist or pentecostal-style preachers in this country. This is fact and will help to provide you with a limited overview as to how hypnosis is being used. The hypnotist who trained the lawyers makes no secret about it. I've worked in advertising and have seen it firsthand, and I've studied the pentecostal church movement for many years.

Hypnosis, in its simplest form, is a narrowing of the attention span to one thing, and a state of suggestibility. Even the lightest trance, which is only a slight mental/physical relaxation, will cause the listener to absorb what is being said at least twenty times as strongly as he would under normal conditions. For the lawyer this is done with a voice roll. He begins to pace his voice . . . and if a metronome were beating in the background he would be in perfect synchronization. It seems as if he is accentuating every third word or so. He is actually rolling his voice in perfect cadence and the result is hypnotic. If he keeps it at about 45–50 beats a minute, it is not obvious to anyone, but the subconscious minds of his listeners have opened up and are absorbing every word. They are now suggestible. Naturally, the lawyer is going to use it only when he wants the maximum effect—such as in the summation. He will sometimes slow the voice roll down to 30 beats a minute, which actually takes his listeners deeper and makes the suggestion even stronger.

Music is equally effective. Any "repetitive" music with about 30 to 50 beats a minute is hypnotic. If combined with a voice roll in cadence to the music, it becomes even more effective. The result: many highly sophisticated and extremely effective television commercials. You have literally been hypnotised in front of your television set hundreds of times without knowing it. How effectively this was perpetrated depends upon how intently you were watching and your natural hypnotic level. Yes, you were sitting there in the room with your eyes open, aware of everything that was going on around you, but you were "lightly" hypnotised. Think about the products you've picked up in the store, feeling you really "wanted" to try them. Maybe you did, and then again maybe you were *made to feel* that you really wanted to try them.

I feel it is important for everyone to know these facts. Hypnosis should be used therapeutically, or by individuals desiring to program positive change, or to expand awareness . . . and never indirectly or subliminally. The mind control of masses of people is a very real concern. Hitler was a master at it. His early rallies combined the repetitive drum roll music and patterned vocal techniques . . . and it worked. Any government, or movement, is capable of the same thing as long as people are unaware of what is happening. Hitler could have told everyone in the audience to kill themselves and no one would have complied, for it would have been a suggestion in violation of their own self-preservation. But by telling receptive minds, over and over, that he was their savior, they finally came to believe it.

Any time you hear repetitive music, especially combined with the vocal patterns I've described—be wary! Which brings me to the growing charismatic church movement. Fundamentalist preachers will claim up and down that they do not use hypnosis. In fact they condemn it as a "tool of the devil." Yet the musical beat goes on, and repeats, and repeats, and the preacher rolls his voice, emphasizing every few words and the audience falls into a light trance. Now maybe the preachers themselves are unaware of the fact they are using hypnosis and are simply imitating the effective techniques of other preachers they have observed. If this is the case, somebody back there knew what he was doing and certainly initiated a successful movement. I am inclined, though, to believe that they know exactly what they are doing and the movement is guilty of being that which it condemns and is so fearful of.

I've explained these things so that you will realize that you're not as unfamiliar with hypnosis as you might think you are. Most people simply do not recognize the state of hypnosis. They expect to become unconscious, and unless you are the one in ten who easily achieves the deep-level trance, this is not at all what the experience is like. Chances are you will remain aware of everything going on around you. This does not mean you are not hypnotised; it simply means you are experiencing a hypnotic level somewhere between a light and medium trance. And believe me that is all that is necessary to reprogram the subconscious mind. It is different for everyone, but normally as you are conditioned you continue to go a little deeper each time you go into hypnosis until your "natural" level is attained.

Anyone can become a good self-hypnosis subject, just as anyone can learn to meditate if they are willing to work at it. The state of consciousness achieved is actually identical—although most individuals who use meditation would disagree, claiming their pathway to be a pure form of achieving enlightenment. To me the difference is quite simple. In meditation you wait for something to happen. In self-hypnosis you decide what you want and cause it to happen.

There are numerous books on the market that profess to teach self-hypnosis. The problem with most of them is that they attempt to fill an entire book with a concept and technique that is easily communicated within a few pages. This unnecessary complication may help justify the cost of the lengthy book, but it also tends to confuse and discourage many people.

Years ago I purchased such a volume and studied it carefully before attempting to apply the techniques. When I finally felt I'd digested the knowledge and began to work with the outlined methods, I was terribly disappointed. It didn't work. I did everything the author told me to do, but nothing seemed to be happening. The writer had built it up to be a very special experience and I felt cheated and thought myself incapable of self-hypnosis.

In retrospect, I realize that of course it was working. I was expecting "something to happen," but this simply is not what the experience is like. I should have continued to work with it at the time, but the author didn't point out the facts that might have made the book less glamorous, but more effective.

CREATING YOUR OWN REALITY
Step 1

Decide exactly what you want—the goal you wish to accomplish. All the known facts regarding your goal should be assembled and fully examined. The argument for and against each aspect should be considered. So think very carefully about how you will use your programming time. Be careful—often what we think of as positive is actually negative. The individual who prays for his country to win the war is actually practicing black magic, for in so doing he is praying for the other side to lose. Any time you think, pray, meditate or use self-hypnosis towards a goal that would be harmful to anyone else it is the "black" use of a very real power.

Remember, you can create anything you want in life if you are willing to pay the price . . . and there is a price. Give a good deal of consideration to what the full price might be. As an example: The goal of fame and money carries with it burdens of responsibility and notoriety that you cannot imagine until you are there. Constant intrusions and lack of privacy. An image-trap that often does not allow you to be yourself, etc.

Write down your goal or goals in the form of a self-hypnosis suggestion. Define it clearly as *a positive, accomplished fact.* By communicating the goal as an accomplished fact your subconscious mind is able to comprehend the goal fully and immediately begin to work towards bringing it into reality.

Many people work at their goals by saying to themselves, "I am going to do it, I know I can and I am going to accomplish this goal." The result is, more often than not, nonachievement and continued problems and hang-ups. Voluntary action can be easily inhibited by systematic thinking. In lecturing to groups I have often used a simple example to illustrate this point. Pick up a pencil and hold it between your thumb and index finger. Now begin to think, "I am going to drop it, I am going to drop it, I am going to drop it" . . . over and over. Now while you are *fully concentrating* upon the phase, "I'm going to drop it," try to drop the pencil. It cannot be done. No matter how hard you try, you will be unable to let go of the pencil while you are using your mental energy on, "I'm going to drop it," because you are really concentrating on the future. Not until you send the message, "Drop it!" from your brain to your fingers will you be able to let go of the pencil. You cannot say, "I am going to accomplish this goal." You must say, "I have accomplished this goal." "I think only positive thoughts," or "I am a great tennis player" . . . even if you have just picked up a tennis racquet for the first time. The more the subconscious hears, "great tennis player," the harder it works to bring the programmed goal into reality.

You can change your life and create your own reality if you set realistic goals and then proceed towards them in a positive way. Change does take time and hypnosis is not a magic wand, but if you are willing to *continually* work towards a particular goal, by using self-hypnosis at least once a day, you *will* achieve the desired results. Remember, you will get back what you put forth—so you must have the patience and discipline to continue to work with this technique over as long a period of time as is necessary. The bigger the goal, the longer it may take.

Once your hypnotic ability is well-developed, you can also use it to accomplish some things immediately. Examples: alleviating a headache, drawing in desired energy, concentration, etc.

One of the most important things to remember in working with self-hypnosis is to concentrate your energy on only one thing, or a couple of related things at one time. In other words, if you use the time to formulate a suggestion such as the following, it would water down all of the suggestions and you would probably accomplish nothing: "I am now going to achieve monetary success, and I will become a better tennis player, and I will reduce my smoking and eat less between meals." Don't try it—you will simply be wasting your time.

If you are willing to work at it, you can literally program yourself to any degree you desire. Everyone has heard of the dog trained to salivate at the sound of a bell. You have the ability with self-hypnosis to program yourself to this extent. I'm sure that is not your goal, but it makes my point.

Remember, in writing out your suggestions, that they must be positive. If, for example, you go into hypnosis and say, "I want to get rid of the headache . . . the headache is going away," you are actually programming yourself negatively, and believe me, the

231

headache won't go away. The word "headache" itself is a negative. The proper way is to concentrate upon the desired end result: "I will awaken with my head feeling clear. My head will feel very good when I awaken relaxed and refreshed." (NOTE: Self-hypnosis should only be used to alleviate pain when you can understand why you have the pain. Pain is nature's way of telling us something is wrong. A tension headache is one thing, but a continuing stomach ache could be appendicitis.)

Step 2

Now letter the key words of your suggestion on a piece of paper and stick them up in an obvious place where you will see them several times a day. "I will think only positive thoughts," for instance. Every time you see it your subconscious is receiving reinforcement.

Step 3

The next step is to either memorize the following technique or make a tape recording of it. This is actually a script and I will explain it in detail in the following step. (Speak slowly and rhythmically.)

"I have now completed my deep breathing and my body is beginning to relax. The relaxing power is coming into my feet . . . They are relaxing . . . and my lower legs are relaxing . . . and my upper legs are now relaxing. I can feel the relaxing power taking over my feet and lower legs and upper legs . . . and now the relaxing power is coming into the fingers of my hands . . . and my hands are relaxing . . . and my forearms are beginning to relax . . . just completely relaxed . . . and my upper arms are relaxing . . . and my hands and forearms and upper arms are just completely relaxed and now the relaxing power is beginning to come into the base of my spine and it is moving slowly . . . slowly . . . up my spine and into the back of my neck and my shoulder muscles . . . Just completely relaxed and the relaxing power is moving up the back of my neck and into my scalp . . . relaxing my scalp . . . and it is draining down into my facial muscles . . . and my facial muscles are completely relaxed . . . and my jaw is relaxed . . . I'm allowing a little space between my teeth . . . and my throat is relaxed. My entire body is now relaxed all over in every way. All tensions are gone from my body and mind and I'm beginning to go into a deep hypnotic sleep . . . and as I do I feel a bright white light coming down from above. . . . It is entering the top of my head and is flowing through my entire body and mind . . . and the light is now concentrating around my heart area . . . and it is emerging from the area of my heart to completely surround my body with a protective, magnetic aura of pure white light. . . . I see it and create it in my mind and thus it becomes real . . . I am totally protected . . . totally protected and only my own Guides and Masters and highly evolved and loving entities who mean me well will be able to influence me in any way while I am in this deep hypnotic sleep . . . deep hypnotic sleep . . . and I'm going deeper and deeper asleep . . . and I'm going deeper and deeper asleep . . . number 7, deeper, . . . deeper . . . deeper . . . down . . . down . . . down . . . number 6 . . . deeper . . . deeper . . . deeper . . . down . . . down . . . down . . . number 5 . . . deeper . . . deeper . . . deeper . . . down . . . down . . . down . . . number 4 . . . deeper . . . deeper . . . deeper . . . down . . . down . . . down . . . number 3 . . . deeper . . . deeper . . . deeper . . . down . . . down . . . down . . . number 2 . . . deeper . . . deeper . . . deeper . . . down . . . down . . . down . . . number 1 . . . I am now in a deep hypnotic sleep, and in a moment I am going to go even deeper . . . but first I am going to imagine a totally peaceful situation in my mind. . . . I will create it in every detail and will mentally become part of this peaceful situation. (One minute of silent time here to imagine the situation.) All

233

right, I am now going to go much deeper into this peaceful, relaxing hypnotic sleep. . . . On the count of one I will be in the deepest possible hypnotic sleep . . . far, far deeper than I have ever been before . . . (Repeat the seven backwards count down.) I am now in the deepest possible hypnotic sleep and each time I hypnotise myself I will go deeper than the time before. I am now going to give myself positive suggestions which are my reality. I absolutely have the power and ability to create my own reality and this is my reality."

(At this point you will insert your own suggestions. Make sure that they are well worded and repetitive so that the subconscious receives them from different perspectives.)

Example: "I now think positive thoughts about everything and everyone . . . and in so doing my life has become so much more positive . . . regardless of the situation, I've learned to cancel out all negative fear thoughts and replace them with love thoughts. This has changed my life. I now fully realize that I create my own reality and by thinking positively I am creating a life of inner harmony and success and happiness. I feel the harmony. . . . I feel the inner peace . . . . and throughout each and every day I retain and strengthen the inner harmony through my own positive thoughts. From this moment on I think only positive, love-based thoughts." (Understand that you can direct this form of positive programming into a special area such as your marital relationship, an unpleasant office situation, etc.)

(Now continue with the script.) "This is my reality . . . . my self-created reality . . . and I am now going to use a few moments to visualize in vivid detail imagined situations that illustrate my new reality." (Three to four minutes of silence.)

(At this point use fantasy to create situations in your mind that will reinforce your suggestions. Remember that the subconscious can't tell the difference between fantasy and reality, so this use of positive affirmation is a primary programming tool. If your primary goal is to improve your marital relationship, imagine your husband doing something, or saying something, that really irritates you, but in fantasy you respond to him with love and nonjudgment. Then visualize the two of you in very happy and loving situations. Create many such situations and try to create new ones each and every time you use hypnosis. Make them as real as you can, creating every detail of these mental motion pictures. At least three or four minutes should be used in this way.)

(Script.) "I have just seen my own reality . . . this is my reality . . . inner harmony is my natural state of being. All right, I am now going to wake myself up. . . . I will awaken feeling as if I'd taken a nice refreshing nap . . . my head will be clear and I will think and act with calm self-assurance . . . feeling good all over . . . feeling glad to be alive. . . . On the count of five I will open my eyes and be wide awake . . . . number 1 . . . number 2 . . . number 3 . . . number 4 . . . number 5. Wide awake . . . wide awake!"

Step 4

You could have been lying down with your eyes closed and simply thought these words to yourself, or you could have spoken them into a tape recorder and then laid down and turned on the player, listening to your own words and following the instructions. I like the tape player because the consistency tends to intensify the suggestions. Plus, once you've gone to the initial effort it makes it very easy to follow through on your reprogramming.

Now let me explain the process in logical order. I will write this section as if you have made a tape.

DEEP BREATHING

Yoga or meditative breathing should be used to relax your body and mind prior to hypnosis. Take the position you will use in hypnosis (sitting or lying down). Set your tape player beside you so it is only a matter of reaching over to turn it on. Now take a very deep breath . . . then let it out very slowly between slightly parted lips. When you think the breath is all the way out, push your stomach in to push out even more air. Take at least five to ten of these deep breaths before turning on the tape. NOTE: If you have a health problem, or it is undesirable to use deep breathing for any reason, simply lie down and relax, breathing normally for several minutes prior to beginning hypnosis. In working with thousands of people in group hypnosis using the deep-breathing technique I have never had anyone hyperventilate (uncontrolled rapid breathing resulting in the decrease of carbon dioxide in the blood). But should this by any chance occur, a paper bag should be placed over your head, which will cause you to rebreathe your own breath and quickly alleviate the problem.

When you have completed relaxation, or deep breathing, make sure you are comfortable; then simply click on your tape player and close your eyes. The tape will instruct you from that time on.

IMPORTANT

Remember, most people do not recognize the state of hypnosis. They expect to become unconscious, and this is simply not what the experience is like. You will probably be aware of everything that is going on in the room and you will hear any sounds you would normally hear if you were simply lying there with your eyes closed. Don't expect to feel much physical sensation, especially at first. After using the tape for a few days you may feel a tingle, or extreme relaxation, or a heavy feeling in your arms, hands, legs and feet. Some people cease to feel their body at all after they are hypnosis-conditioned. You will become a totally hypnosis-conditioned subject within two to four weeks if you use your tape once a day.

HOW TO HELP YOURSELF BECOME A
BETTER SELF-HYPNOSIS SUBJECT

First of all, try to keep your full attention on the sound of your voice on the tape. Everyone's mind will wander, but as soon as you realize this is happening, bring your full attention back to the sound of your voice.

The best hypnotic subject is one who can visualize, or use imagination or fantasy to see a situation in his or her mind. The better you can use your own mind to imagine ("imagine-in"), the easier you can go into a hypnotic trance.

Please do not make judgments about what you are experiencing initially. Simply flow with what is happening. Anyone can become a highly developed self-hypnosis subject, but overanalyzing can retard your progress.

It is desirable to darken the room, or use a dark sleep mask, when working with hypnosis. This is certainly not necessary, but it does seem to make visualization easier for most people. If you are attempting to see mental pictures, I believe you will agree.

After completing your deep breathing, turn on your tape player. The first instructions are for body relaxation. You can help by "playing the role." Actually "feel" your feet, legs, arms, etc., relaxing.

After the relaxation comes the spiritual protection, which I feel is important. Even if this is not part of your own belief system it is desirable to use this, for it is a good exercise in programming the mind visually.

The next step is the beginning of actual hypnosis induction. Keep your full attention on the sound of your voice, and use your active imagination very, very vividly to visualize yourself in a situation in which you are going down. You will be counting backwards from seven to one and as you do this I want you to see yourself going down. Create a pleasing mental picture.

You could be walking down a forest path, the steps of a building, climbing down rocks to the sea or whatever appeals to you. But do this with as much imagination as you can.

At the induction midpoint you are going to visualize a situation in your own mind that is totally peaceful to you. Once more, use your imagination to re-create an actual situation, or fantasize one in vivid detail. Create everything about this peaceful situation in your mind. See it and feel it . . . become part of it . . . exactly where you are, how you are dressed, how warm or cool it is, and the emotions you are feeling. If there are other individuals in this situation with you, imagine them in every detail.

You will count backwards from seven to one again, visualizing yourself going down. Then simply follow the instructions as I have already related them. That's it. It isn't complicated, or mystical, but it does work. The technique incorporates the ancient methodologies, and contemporary variations such as psycho-cybernetics, only it intensifies them by going straight to the subconscious via this altered state of consciousness.

A FEW IMPORTANT POINTS

1. If you wear contact lenses and would normally remove them before taking a nap, do so before going into self-hypnosis.

2. Do not cross your legs while in hypnosis, for weight is often exaggerated and this illusion of excessive weight can be distracting.

3. If after using your tape for awhile you seem to "trip out" and do not recall what has transpired while you were under hypnosis, reduce the amount of deep breathing prior to going under and use only one series of backward seven countdowns. These instructions relate to the situation of you waking up on the count of five, but recalling nothing that has transpired.

4. Body position: Try to pick a time for

hypnosis when you will not be interrupted and a place where it is quiet. You may sit in a comfortable chair or lie down in bed. If sitting, place both feet flat on the floor and your hands on your legs. If lying down, place your hands at your sides.

5. The lying down position is best, but we do not want you to fall into a normal sleep. Avoid using your tape when you are very tired. The tape will condition your subconscious mind, and you *do not* want to condition it to fall asleep when you go into hypnosis. If you should fall asleep two times while in the prone position, continue further sessions in a sitting position for a few days. If you don't do this, your subconscious will actually become programmed, very quickly, to fall asleep every time you use the tape. There is no danger in falling asleep while using the tape (not awakening on the count of 5); it is only the sleep habit pattern established in the subconscious, which is to be avoided.

6. Many people are afraid that if they go into hypnosis they might not wake up . . . or if the tape player broke in the middle of a self-hypnosis session they would remain in a trance forever. Not so! If this were to happen, you would do one of two things. First and most likely, you would simply open your eyes and wake up. I would suggest, if this were the case, to simply count yourself up as you do on the tape. "On the count of 5 I will open my eyes and be wide awake, 1,2,3,4,5." If the tape player broke while you were in a trance and you were tired, you could very well go off into a normal, natural sleep, waking up when you had enough rest . . . just as you normally do in the morning.

7. More than one person at a time can work with the tape. It is ideal for a couple, or several people to work together on reprogramming, if they can all agree on identical programming. In the area of relationship problems I always en-

239

courage couples to work together—ideally holding hands while in the hypnotic state, for this helps to create a mental bond that continues after the session.

Happy reprogramming and new reality.

CHAPTER 23

SHIELDING AND PROTECTION TECHNIQUES

Psychic attack in its classic form is voodoo, witchcraft or any form of sorcery in which an individual, or group of individuals, project purposeful and calculated malevolent thoughts (power) to another. That may sound melodramatic, but it is real. It does happen today, and if you're the intended victim you should be aware of how to reject or reflect such aggressions.

Mind expansion has become a national movement. Millions are learning about their psychic powers, how to concentrate and direct thought, and to create desired realities with the power of their mind. Major sports stars, in many cases, are publicly proclaiming that they owe their winning to such self-techniques. As more people learn to use these powers we will see more misuse.

Psychic attack in its "unintentional" form is simply the negative thoughts of one person toward another. Anger, fear, jealous or vindictive thoughts about someone are actually projected to that person. The degree the other person is subconsciously affected by, or accepts, this negativity is probably in direct ratio to his inner harmony, although this might not be the case with someone with high empathic receiving abilities.

As I've already discussed in detail, *we are mind.*

Mind is the ultimate power, so to underestimate its potential is quite foolish.

Often while lecturing, to illustrate the power of perception, I tell a true story of J. Allen Boone, the famous author and Hollywood animal trainer.

Boone claims his successful career was based upon his ability to communicate mentally with animals. He projected his thoughts to them and used developed techniques to "open" to receive their feelings and emotions. In some cases literal telepathic conversational links seem to have resulted, and he wrote in detail of allowing a pet monkey to teach him techniques to "examine the hearts" of people.

While resting alone one day in a jungle clearing, Boone watched a monkey swing out of the trees and drop to the center of the clearing, where it sat down to observe him. He knew from his experience with the monkey that he was being "examined," through a ceremonial practice, and he began to flow with the situation. They were contacting each other as fellow states-of-consciousness rather than as mere physical forms. It lasted several minutes, then the monkey stopped, looked all around him, and as he did the clearing exploded with wild monkeys. Young, old, big and small, it was raining monkeys and they seemed to have come to perform and play for Boone's benefit.

The mental examination had evidently yielded favorable facts. A genuine admiration and respect of monkeys had been perceived and the scout had given his invisible stamp of approval. For several hours Boone watched the pageant and enjoyed the mental exchange; then with startling abruptness every monkey stopped what he was doing and looked to the south. A moment later, obviously motivated by fear and panic, they all stampeded out of the clearing—heading north.

Boone wanted to know why, so he waited and waited. It was three hours later that five men walked into the clearing carrying rifles. Two were American sportsmen and three attendants. All were surprised to see each other, but the sportsmen explained that they were traveling all over the world, shooting various kinds of animals to have them stuffed for exhibition purposes. They'd come to the clearing because it was known as a monkey hangout, yet they hadn't seen a single one this day.

Boone kept quiet about his experiences there, but questioned the men as to when they'd started the morning's hunt. "Exactly three hours ago," one of the sportsmen replied, looking at his watch.

At the precise moment the hunters picked up their guns and headed for the clearing, three hours walking distance away, every monkey had perceived the danger and fled in the opposite direction. The men were mentally working themselves up for the hunt, projecting discordant mental vibrations—bad-intentioned and destructive thoughts. Monkey murder was rumbling in their hearts and minds with every step.

Their deadly thinking, which was projecting far ahead of them, crashed into the joy-filled vibrations of the monkeys. Although the clash was only mental, it had a terrific outward impact. Immediately upon receiving the telepathic broadcast of the hunters, the monkeys disappeared.

Ask any deer hunter about all the deer disappearing on the first day of the hunting season. Is it simply because they come to fear the sounds of the guns? I don't think so.

Thoughts can be transmitted; that is a provable fact. In sending the receiving tests with five-day seminar participants I've often had eighty and ninety percent success results by using hypnotic techniques to expand their belief system for a few moments in time. I tell them, "You can do it," and because they *believe they can do it,* under hypnosis, they do it. In reality they don't need hypnosis at all; it is simply that they can't trust the familiar portion of their mind called the "conscious."

We have larger minds than monkeys, and certainly any "monkey ability" lies within that ninety-five percent of our mind which is not normally used. I don't, nor does anyone I'm aware of, know exactly how this transmission occurs: telepathic, telekinetic, teleaudio, sonic, electromagnetic, or animal magnetic. I'll leave that one to the scientists. The fact is *thoughts can help, heal or harm.*

If you want to rise above karmic effects with someone else, send them thoughts of love every time you think of them. Silently say, "I love you," and imagine that love flowing from your heart to that person, and mentally see the person surrounded in a glow of white light because of it. This is the standard practice of many metaphysicians who desire to turn a negative interpersonal relationship into a positive one. I've often advised it to soothe the wounds in a divorce situation. Self-hypnosis can be used as a mental technique to concentrate such projections and accelerate the change. Never use it in an attempt to manipulate the reality of another person, for this could be karmically destructive to you.

So often someone will tell me, "I want to get back together with him, so I'm going to use these powers to pull him to me. I'll program that goal, and I'll use positive affirmations of him and me together to bring it into reality."

"That is a psychic attack, or the use of witchcraft," I'll respond.

"But then I'll be happy again!"

"I doubt, if you use such technique to achieve the togetherness, that you will be happy," I tell them. "It could very well be worse than ever before. The real goal, or final desired end result, is a happy relationship with a man you love, is that correct?"

"Well, yeah . . . if I could really be happy with anyone else."

"Then program the goal of a happy relationship. Don't resrict the goal by saying, 'It has to be Jack,' or 'He has to be six foot, have black curly hair and be as handsome as a Greek god.' "

If you really want to get back together with Jack, I would advise that you send Jack love, without manipulative motives. Use the mind power techniques to change yourself in a positive way. Then if it does work out that the two of you are to share a relationship, it will be the result of a natural harmony.

SPIRITUAL PROTECTION TECHNIQUES

In the last chapter as part of the hypnosis tape, I described the visualization of white light surrounding your body. This is the basis of most metaphysical protection.

You can use it with self-hypnosis, or meditation for intensification, or simply by thought projection for a "quick hit." Most everyone I know "thinks" white light around their car when they climb into it, and they surround their apartment or home with white light when they leave. Often if a worry thought comes to me about one of my children, I will quickly, mentally, send white light to surround them.

But let's assume for a moment that you are dealing with a very real situation of classic, or unintentional, psychic attack. Maybe you only suspect such a situation. The symptoms are depression without apparent reason. Inability to think or concentrate effectively. Thoughts you feel to be alien to your normal life pattern. Unexplainable mental or physical pain. A negative change in your feelings towards another person for no apparent reason.

Protection Step 1: Light three white candles and decide on a place where you will either sit or lie down. One candle should stand two feet in front of you (or from your feet if you are lying down) and the others should each be two feet from each side of your body.

Protection Step 2: Go into hypnosis or meditation. Use the initial protection technique, as I have already described, then go ahead and complete the induction —taking yourself very deep.

Protection Step 3: (Say this to yourself, or use it as the basis of a tape script.) "In the name of the positive powers of the universe I call upon my own Guides and Masters to come and be with me at this time. . . . Help me . . . add your strength to my own . . . be with me now. (Pause.) My Guides and Masters are now with me and I am totally protected from any negativity . . . from the adverse thoughts of others through psychic attack, or from forces beyond the physical realms. To begin I am going to release all negativity from my own body . . . through this ancient and effective technique I will now rid myself of all negativity . . . number 1, number 2, number 3. (On the count of three you are to blow out a very deep breath, actually making an audible noise while doing so. Repeat this process three times and as you do, "feel" the negativity leaving your body and mind.) All negativity has now left my body and mind and I am beginning to expand the white light that already surrounds me. This protective aura of magnetic white God light is now beginning to expand . . . I see it in my mind . . . my own Guides and Masters are helping to create a protective magnetic bubble of pure white . . . expanding . . . expanding . . . the God light which will totally protect me from any negativity being projected at me. With the power of my own mind and the power of my own will, and with the help of the unseen who love me, I have created a totally effective force field . . . a magnetic, protectory bubble through which only good can penetrate . . . through which only love can penetrate. Any outside negativity being directed at me will simply bounce off this protective aura of white light. I am now surrounded by a bubble which totally protects me and all negativity will now bounce off this protectory bubble like a mirror. It will bounce off and I ask that it bounce out into outer space, where it will dissipate harmlessly. I now want to send love to all who send me negativity . . . love is the most powerful force in the universe . . . it will mitigate and put an end to the misuse of power on the part of others . . . so I am sending the love . . . I feel it manifesting around my heart area . . . and it is now flowing from me . . . I feel it happening . . . I see it happening . . . I'm sending love."

(End of script)

You can add on to this in any way you desire. For example if you feel the psychic attack is being projected from your husband, visualize the love now being projected to him. If you desire to protect others whom you love, see the light go out to them and see them surrounded with it. There is certainly no limit to the ways love and light can be projected.

I've seen people literally change their lives overnight by using this technique. For others it builds with each successive use. It is the only metaphysical area in which I advise the use of ritual symbols. The reason for the candles, in addition to the spiritual qualities of white, is that they quickly intensify the subconscious programming trigger. Candles = protection and the computer is programmed for protection.

One of my subjects had to use this technique three times a day to ward off an attack, but in so doing her health returned and she was able to maintain her job once again. Her personal test would be the decision to reflect the negativity back to the purposeful sender, or to use love to conquer the problem.

Negativity is ideally "sent out into space where it will dissipate harmlessly." But you can use the bubble as a mirror to reflect the projection back to the sender, causing him an immediate balance. In this situation you have responded to mental violence with mental violence, and another human being will be harmed because of it. Thus it may be your karma. It is far better to let the natural balance work itself out.

SHIELDING TECHNIQUES

If you have empathic abilities and temporarily do not want to receive from others, I would advise the same form of mental projections, but also develop a "conditioned response word," such as *shield*. Use self-hypnosis to program that every time you say the word "shield" you will instantly surround yourself with a transparent shield that will protect you from all external mental input. Tell yourself, "When I say the word 'shield' I will become relaxed and at ease, and a very real mental shield will surround my mind. The thoughts, feelings and emotions of other people will be unable to touch me until I open to them once more."

Use positive affirmation programming as well as the words. See yourself in the midst of angry people, without being affected by their lack of balance. See yourself offering advice to someone in need without being adversely affected by the contact. The more you practice this technique, the more effective it will become.

CHAPTER 24

A LOVE STORY

In this volume I've introduced many new psychic metaphysical concepts, and some case history evidence that doesn't fit into the classic philosophy. Accept none of it as dogma, but only as research resulting in concepts to be further explored.

The material may have given a few people so much to think about that they became overpowered by the entire overview. If this is the case, I feel I may have done a great disservice, for indeed metaphysics is not complicated. It all boils down to one word—*Love*. Notice that I spelled that with a capital "L" which to me indicates love far beyond that experienced in interpersonal relationships. To begin, it means self-love, which if fully developed would be the *inner harmony* I've discussed so much. Naturally, it includes the love of your mate, and family and friends, but it ideally goes beyond that to encompass the totality. Love of the part and the whole, the cell and the body, you as an individual and you as all that is.

To capsulize my entire belief in the simplest statement: *"You purposely chose to explore your present potential to perfect your ability to Love."* That covers it all, and Elena and John Sherry are a perfect example:

ELENA AND JOHN SHERRY

"I can't even imagine what we must have gone through in our past lives to have had to fight as hard as we did together in this life," Elena told me.

"Once we made it we've held on for dear life and enjoyed every minute of thirteen years of marriage," John injected.

"Every minute?" Elena questioned with one raised eyebrow.

"I guess there were some bad minutes, but in looking back I sure wouldn't trade any of them in!" he stated emphatically.

I'd met the Sherrys only a few days before at a friend's home in Los Angeles. John was thirty-eight, Elena thirty-six. They were warm, handsome people and obviously very happy together. I'd accepted an invitation to have lunch with them at a seafood restaurant on the Santa Monica pier.

"What was so hard about getting together in the first place?" I asked.

"Well, first of all, I'm Jewish," John began, "and Elena is Catholic. You can imagine how thrilled both of our families were about that one. We originally planned to be married in 1959, but the pressures that both of our families brought to bear, were . . . well, unbearable. We buckled. Elena went off to school and I joined the army."

"But we stayed in constant contact," Elena said. "I wrote him enough letters for three lifetimes. We planned to be married then in 1962, but John was sent to Viet Nam as a 'Military advisor.' I got a job as a secretary here in L. A. and settled into waiting until he came home."

"It was during that time that Elena found out she had lupus (a tuberculosis of the skin). The doctor told her that it was incurable, and normally fatal, and there was very little that could be done to even treat

250

the symptoms. But that wasn't about to stop this lady of mine."

"I simply wasn't going to miss my chance to marry John. That was all there was to it. I'd take long walks on the beach at night and tell myself 'Get well, you silly goose, get well.' There was a big dark patch of skin that was spreading from a point on my neck. Then it just started to fade away. The doctor couldn't believe it. I couldn't believe it, but it was true. Of course, by then John was home. He'd been wounded in the head and was in the Veterans Hospital here for months before he was released."

I was aware that John had lost over forty percent of his vision and there was no way to know how long he could retain what remained.

"When did you finally get married?" I asked.

"Nineteen-sixty-four. John sported a beautiful white bandage. It looked like I was marrying one of those Hindus," Elena laughed. "We probably should have had children," she continued, "but I didn't know when lupus might reappear, and we've always known that John might lose his sight, so we just decided to live every day for all it was worth . . . enjoying each other. It was a good decision."

"And you really want to be hypnotically regressed into a past life when you've got this one handled so well?" I questioned.

"I don't," John said. "Elena is fascinated with philosophies and probabilities and you in particular, Richard. Your last book made her feel good. But I warn you ahead of time, if she comes up with a past life in which I am some grand hero, I will forever accuse her of fantasizing it."

ELENA
Regression Session

Hypnosis induced, spiritual protection invoked and the following instructions were given: "If you and your present husband John have been together before

251

in a past life, or past lives, I would like you now to return to a meaningful situation that transpired in another time and place."

Elena initially saw herself as a Catholic nun living in the mid-eighteen hundreds in France. Her present husband John was Father Joseph. She described life in the convent/church environment, and explained that there was exceptionally intense political opposition to the church at that time (a fact that proved to be historically true). The following portion of the transcript from the regression is pertinent to Sister Ruth's relationship with Father Joseph.

Q. Well, tell me how you feel about him. It seems that you must respect him very much by what you have told me.
A. Oh yes, very much.
Q. You're in love with him, aren't you?
A. I love Father, like I love everyone, but I cannot be "in love" with him.
Q. You're not supposed to, but I believe you are.
A. I can't be . . . I can't . . . (She begins to cry softly.)
Q. It's all right . . . I think it's beautiful, and I won't tell anyone.
A. What am I going to do? Thank you. Thank you. I love him so much, but it is so wrong.
Q. It is only wrong if you feel it is wrong. I don't feel it is wrong.
A. Oh, but it is. You shouldn't say things like that. I mustn't love Father Joseph like this. I must pray harder to be alleviated of this burden.

Sister Ruth lived out her life in the convent, outwardly controlling her emotions. From what she told me, I believe that Father Joseph shared similar feelings, but handled the situation in the same way. Their love had carried forward, but maybe their guilt had too. Possibly the feeling that it was wrong to love each other manifested in subconsciously created prob-

252

lems that would normally have averted the culmination of the relationship. Yet love did win out and that was all that was important to the Sherrys now.

Love always wins. Sometimes it just takes a little longer. You can learn to perfect love in this life, or the next one, or maybe the one after that. You came here to go to school and you'll keep trying until you graduate. What are a few lifetimes more or less?

ABOUT THE AUTHOR

Dick Sutphen is a psychic researcher, skilled hypnotist, and lecturer. He has appeared on many major television shows and performed the first nationally broadcast past-life regression on Tom Snyder's NBC *Tomorrow* show. Dick is the author of the best-selling book, *You Were Born Again to Be Together,* and has written numerous metaphysical, nostalgia, and love-poetry books, and produced a line of hypnosis tapes.

He often works with colleges and metaphysical groups and, together with his wife Trenna, conducts past-life regression seminars each year in Scottsdale, Arizona, and various cities around the country.

Sutphen lives in Scottsdale, where he continues to write and conduct his research. Inquiries: Dick Sutphen, Box 4276, Scottsdale, Arizona 85258.

14